The Big Book of Bible Games

Volume I

By
Linda Standke

Cover illustration by
Margo De Paulis

Inside illustrations by
Deb Kirkeeide

Publishers
In Celebration
a division of Instructional fair • TS Denison
Grand Rapids, Michigan 49544

Copyright Notice

Dedication

To my game players: Nick, Danny, Timmy, and Jeffy,
who prompted my enthusiasm with their love for games and
eagerness to learn about Jesus' love. I love you guys.
Mom

Credits:
Author: Linda Standke
Project Director: Sherrill B. Flora
Cover Illustration: Margo De Paulis
Inside Illustrations: Deb Kirkeeide
Typesetting: Deborah McNiff

About the Author:
Linda Standke lives in Bloomington, Minnesota, with her husband, Bill, and their four sons. Linda is an active member in her church. She has served on the Christian Education Committee, directed Preschool Bible School, conducted Preschool Music, taught Sunday School, and was employed as the Coordinator of Children's Ministries. Linda says writing Christian education material "is truly a blessing in my life. To be spreading God's message through my books is fulfilling a dream and an answer to prayer."

Standard Book Number: 1-56822-329-3
SPCN: 990-219-2556
The Big Book of Bible Games—Volume I
Copyright © 1996 by In Celebration™
a division of Instructional Fair • TS Denison
2400 Turner Avenue NW
Grand Rapids, Michigan 49544

All Rights Reserved • Printed in the USA

Introduction

The Big Book of Bible Games has been designed for Christian Schools, Sunday School Programs, Church Retreats, Youth Groups, Vacation Bible Schools, Church Carnivals, Home Educators, Parents, and simply for anyone who loves playing games and learning about God's Word.

Creating these exciting Christian games is easy—everything is included! You will find reproducible patterns, gameboards, playing cards, scorecards, as well as clear and easy-to-follow directions.

People will delight in learning more about the Bible as they play these educational games. "Baseball Bible Trivia," "The Bible Book Spinner Game," and "Who/What Bible Bingo," just to mention several games, will sharpen your knowledge of the Bible while entertaining.

Making these games can be as much fun as playing them. Have the children in your classroom help you, or recruit the help of your own children. Creating these games is a wonderful family project. Store the games in file folders or in cardboard boxes, so that you can enjoy them for years to come!

Table of Contents

Bible Memory

Through pictures or word recognition cards,
children will match Bible knowledge skills as they test their memory.

What you need:
scissors, tagboard, glue

What you do:
Copy, mount on tagboard, and cut out memory cards. You may want to color the Bible Picture Memory Cards or copy them on colored paper (pages 6-12). Copy the word recognition cards on colored paper (pages13-19). Covering with clear contact paper will strengthen the cards and make them last longer.

To play:
Shuffle cards and lay face down on a large playing surface (table top or floor) to form a square.

First player turns over two Bible Memory Cards for all to see—if they match, the player keeps them and takes another turn. When the cards do not match, the player must return the cards to their original spots. Remember, ALL players must see the cards before they are returned to their original spots. Play continues until all of the cards have been paired up and collected. The child with the most pairs wins the game.

Creation	Creation
Adam and Eve	Adam and Eve
Cain and Abel	Cain and Abel
Noah	Noah
Isaac and Rebekah	Isaac and Rebekah

Joseph and his Coat	Joseph and his Coat
Moses and the Burning Bush	Moses and the Burning Bush
The Plagues	The Plagues
The Passover	The Passover
The Exodus	The Exodus

The Ten Commandments	The Ten Commandments
The Golden Calf	The Golden Calf
Job	Job
Daniel and the Lion's Den	Daniel and the Lion's Den
Jonah	Jonah

David and Goliath	David and Goliath
Samson and Delilah	Samson and Delilah
The Baptism of Jesus	The Baptism of Jesus
The Sower and the Seed	The Sower and the Seed
Jesus Feeds 5000	Jesus Feeds 5000

Jesus Walks on Water	Jesus Walks on Water
The Lost Sheep	The Lost Sheep
The Little Children and Jesus	The Little Children and Jesus
The Rich Young Man	The Rich Young Man
The Lord's Supper	The Lord's Supper

The Resurrection	The Resurrection
John the Baptist	John the Baptist
Friends that Lowered their Friend through the Roof	Friends that Lowered their Friend through the Roof
A Man with Leprosy	A Man with Leprosy
Jesus Calms a Storm	Jesus Calms a Storm

The Mustard Seed	The Mustard Seed
Jesus Clears the Temple	Jesus Clears the Temple
Doubting Thomas	Doubting Thomas
Pentecost	Pentecost
Ask, Seek, Knock	Ask, Seek, Knock

Bible Charades

Old and New Testament titles create a fun game for children of all ages.

You will need:
floor space, scissors, clear contact paper, and a timer (watch, egg timer, or sand timer)

What you do:
- Copy and laminate Bible Charade cards. Cut out on the solid lines.
- Divide children into two teams. Decide which team goes first.
- One person draws a Bible Charade card. Set the timer (two minutes maximum) and say "go." The player acts out the words on the card for his/her teammates. The team tries to guess the words the player is acting out. If the team cannot guess, the player may give the title or the other team may guess, whichever you prefer. If the children would like to keep score, a scorekeeper should be designated to keep track of correct answers.

Helpful hints:
To help children who are not familiar with charades, there are some common hand signals that may be used:

tugging of ear = sounds like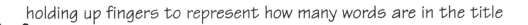

holding up fingers to represent how many words are in the title

holding finger and thumb apart about an inch = small word

laying one, two, or three fingers inside of elbow = number of syllables in the word

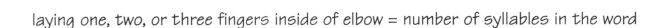

Encourage children to be creative and to have fun.

The Fall of Man	God Sends the Rain
Jacob Wrestles with God	Moses and the Burning Bush
The Plague of Frogs	The Passover
Crossing the Sea	Water from the Rock
The Ten Commandments	The Ark
The Golden Calf	The Bronze Snake

Wandering in the Desert	David and Goliath
Soloman Builds a Temple	Jonah gets Swallowed
Moses in a Basket	A Rainbow in the Sky
Pharoah's Army Drown	Job Suffers
God Answers Prayer	Daniel in the Lion's Den
The Lord is my Strength	Do not Steal

Jesus Wept	The Lost Sheep
Thy Word is a Lamp unto my Feet	Jesus was Born in Bethlehem
Love is Kind	The Rich Man
Jesus Washed Away our Sins	Walking in the Light
Pray Always	Rejoice in the Lord Always
A Woman Lost a Coin	Jesus in the Temple

Jesus Died	Rained 40 Days
Angels Sang	Paul in Prison
John the Baptist	Triumphant Entry (Palm Sunday)
Sower and the Seed	Last Supper
The Hidden Treasure	Jesus is Alive Again
Walk on Water	Zaccheus

Singing in Jail	Love One Another
Jesus loves children	Mary and Martha
Three Wisemen	Man Lowered through Roof
A Boy Shares his Lunch	Ten Lepers
A Star in the East	Holy Spirit
Triune God	Talking Donkey

All ages, 2–20 players

What you need:
markers for Bingo cards—beans, M & M's, small bits of construction paper . . . container for Bingo caller

What you do:
- Copy or cut Bingo cards (pages 27-36), caller's cards (39-40), and master caller card(37-38). You may wish to laminate for strength or copy onto construction paper.
- You may wish to mount the Bingo cards onto colored construction paper for strength and to look more attractive.
- You also may choose to color in your Bingo cards. Be sure the same picture is colored the same on all cards.
- Attaching an envelope to a file folder provides a storage unit for the Bingo cards and caller's cards.

How to play:
- Choose a caller. This person gets the master Bingo card and the caller's cards. Place caller's cards in a container.
- Everyone else receives a Bible bingo card and markers for their card. Be sure everyone puts a marker on the "grace" space, since "grace" is the free space.
- The caller then pulls out a card and calls out, loud and clear, what the picture is (every card contains each picture). Pictures are covered with markers as they are called and the caller covers that picture on the master Bingo card with Caller's card
- Play continues until someone gets five markers in a row—either horizontally, vertically, or diagonally. You may choose black out games four corners, T or L games where markers need to cover appropriate pictures to make those shapes.
- You may wish to have a basket of trinkets to give as prizes when a Bingo has been called.

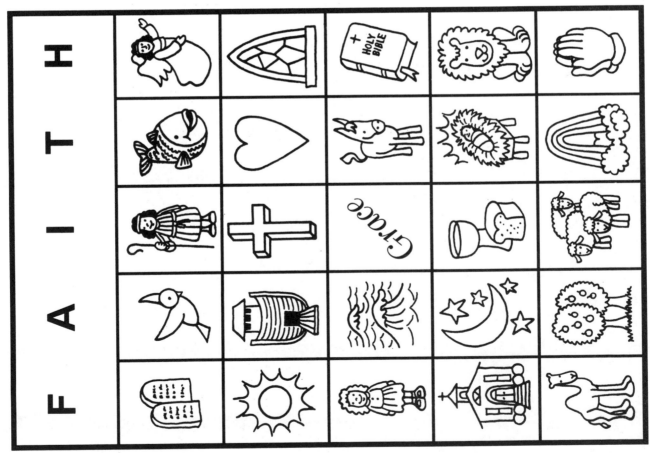

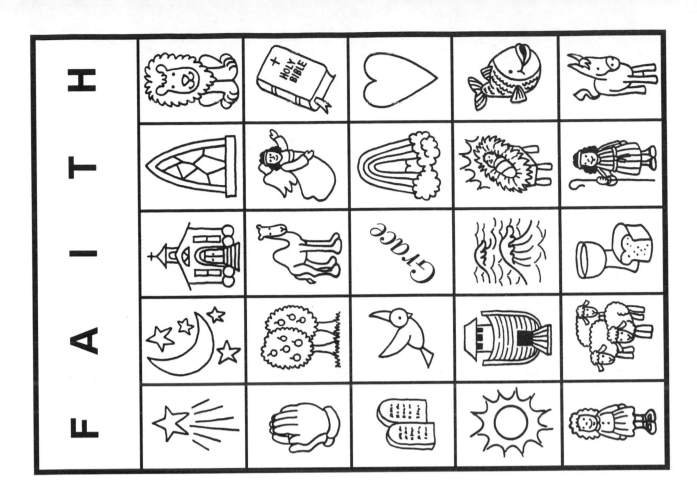

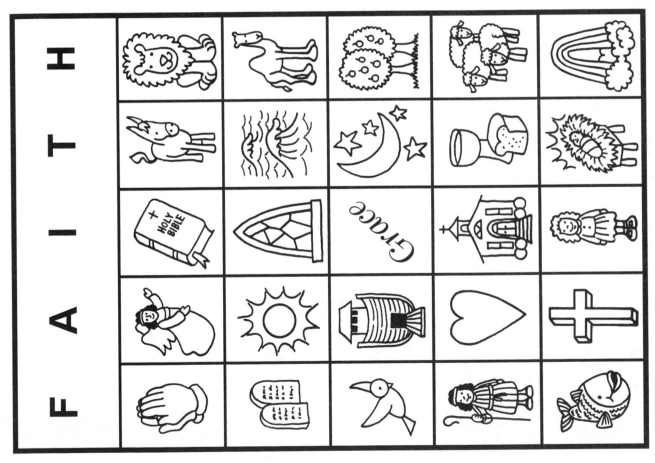

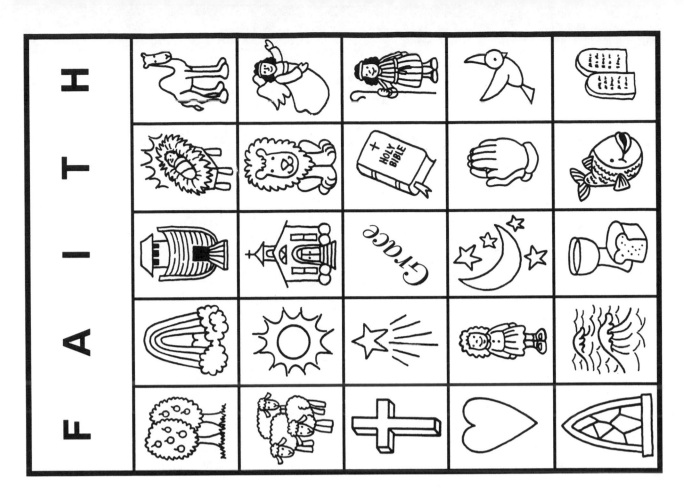

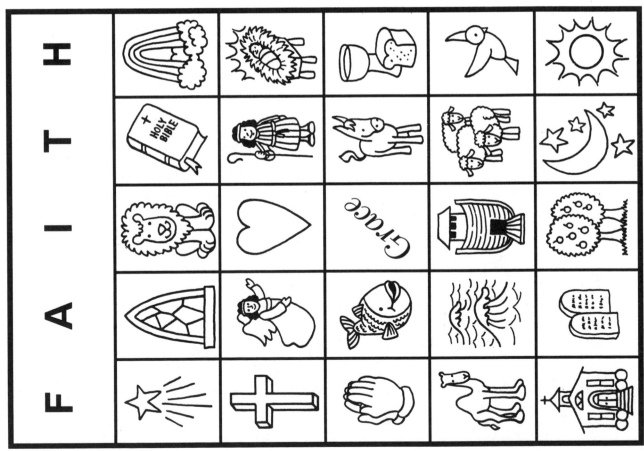

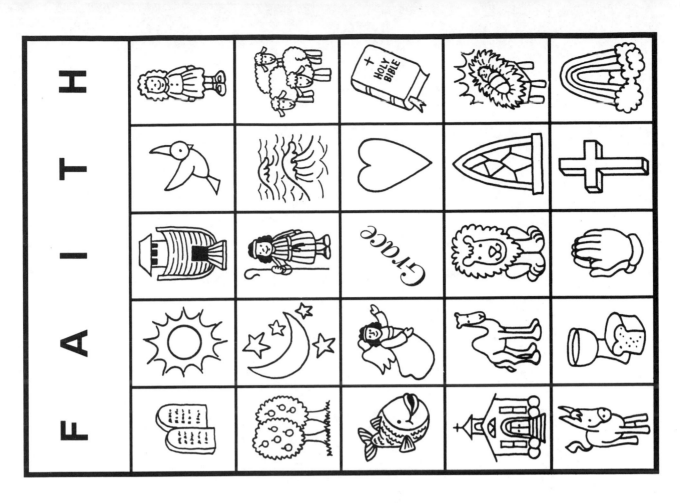

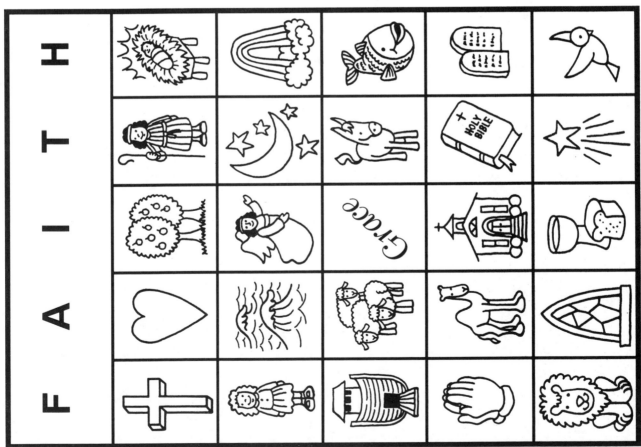

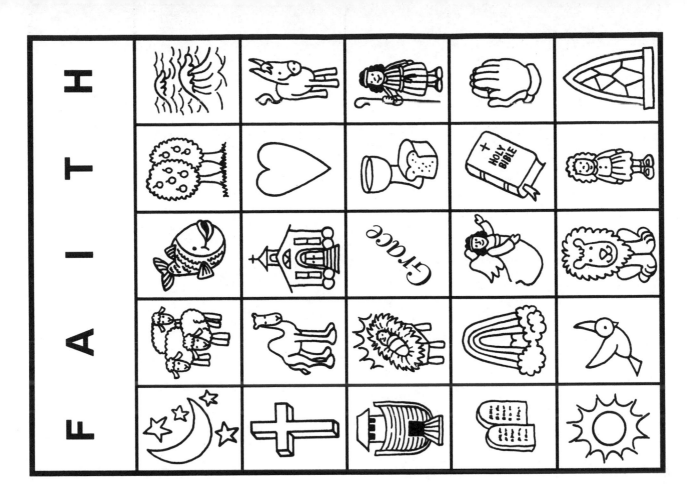

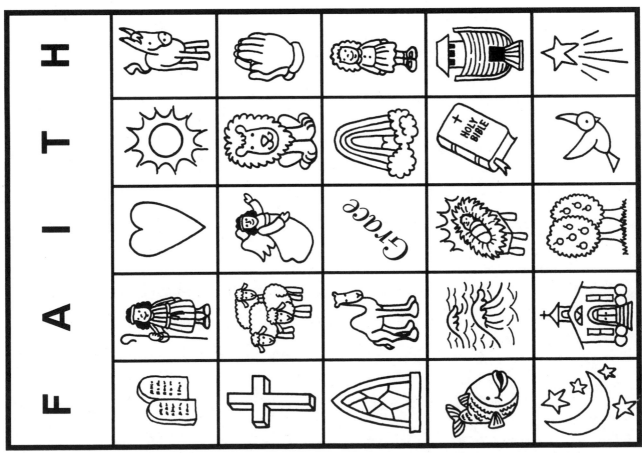

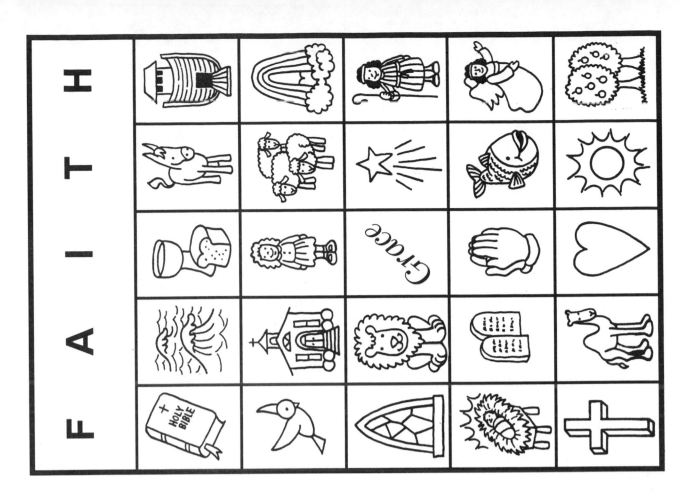

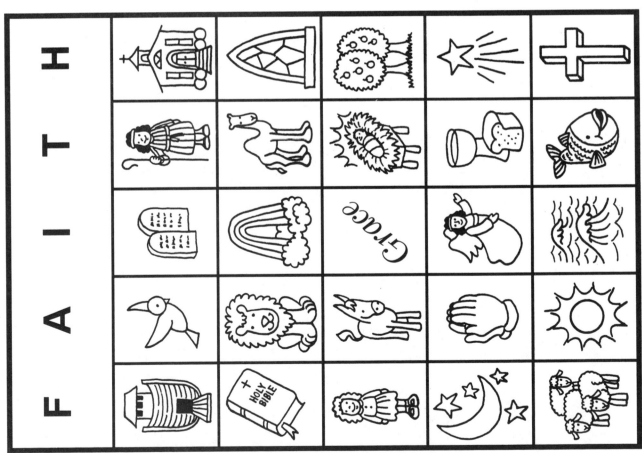

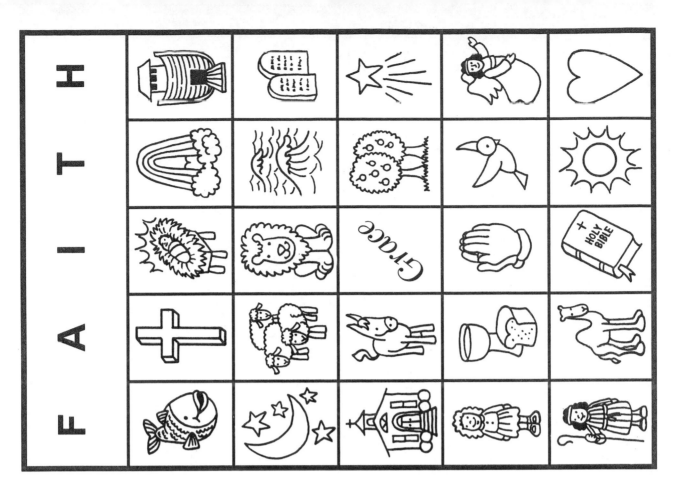

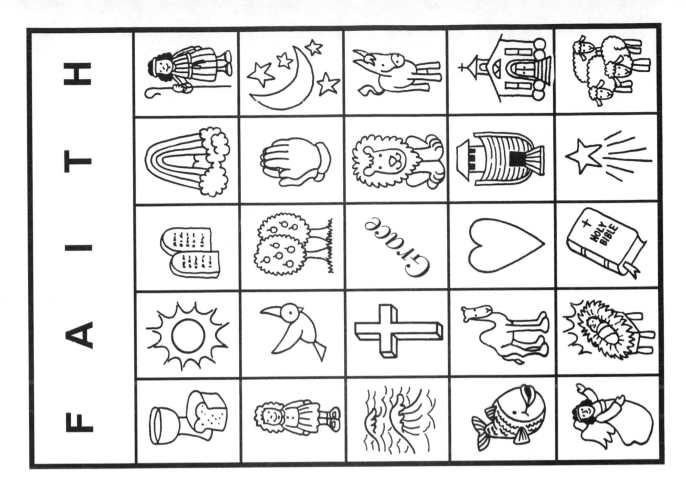

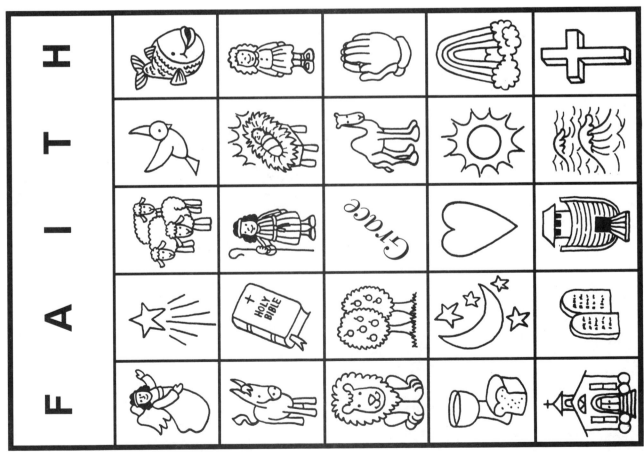

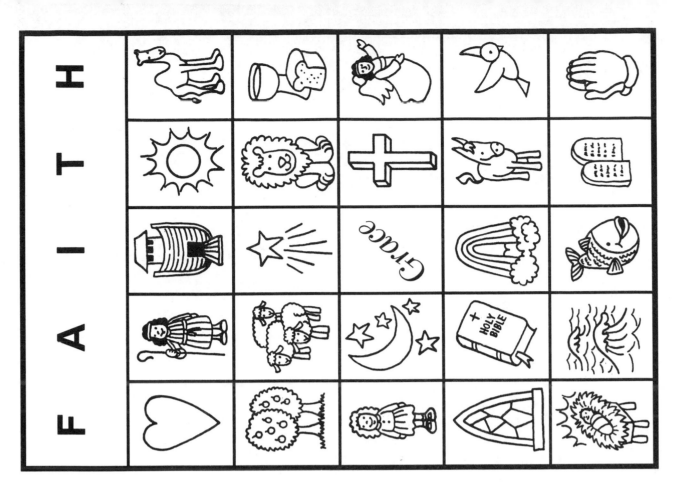

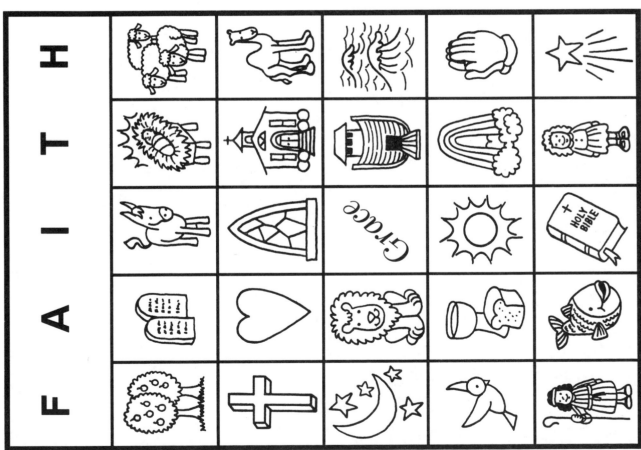

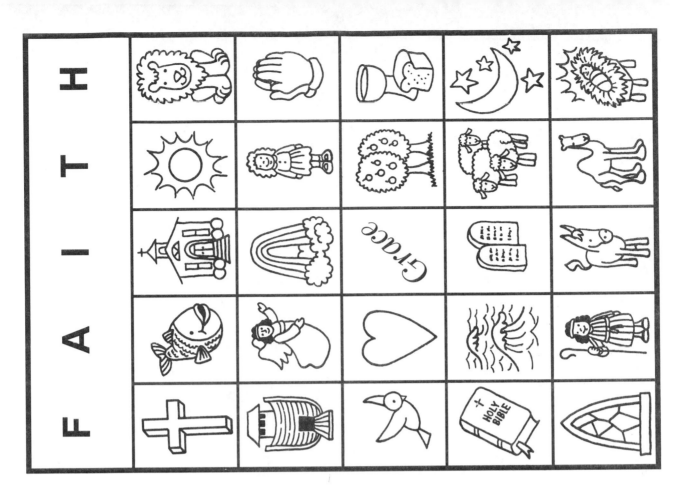

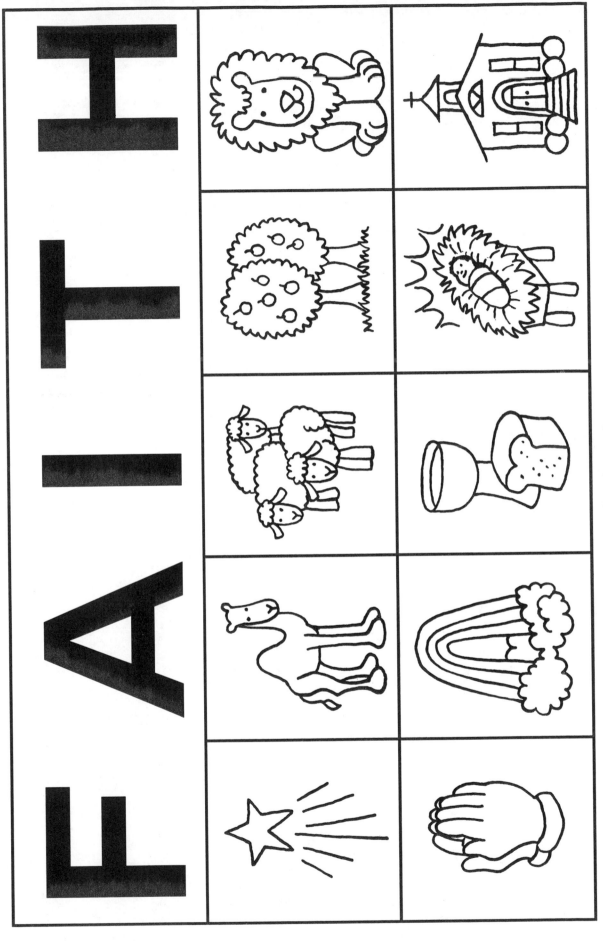

continued on next page

The Big Book of Bible Games—Volume 1

overlap page xx onto this section and glue

Bingo Calling Cards

Action game to reinforce Bible truths.

You will need;
string, paper clips, magnet, dowel or fishing pole

What you do:
- Cut out the fish (pages 42-48)—color if you wish.
- Cover the fish with clear contact paper and mount on tagboard. The fiah could also be copied onto colored construction paper.
- Attach a paper clip to each fish and lay them face down on the floor.
- Create a fishing pole by attaching a magnet to a string and tying it to the end of the dowel rod.

Variations:
After spreading the fish on the floor face down, children "fish them up and:

Preschool—do the action written on fish
Elementary—Look up the in the Bible the verse printed on the fish. Read it aloud, and then do the action.

Fish Patterns

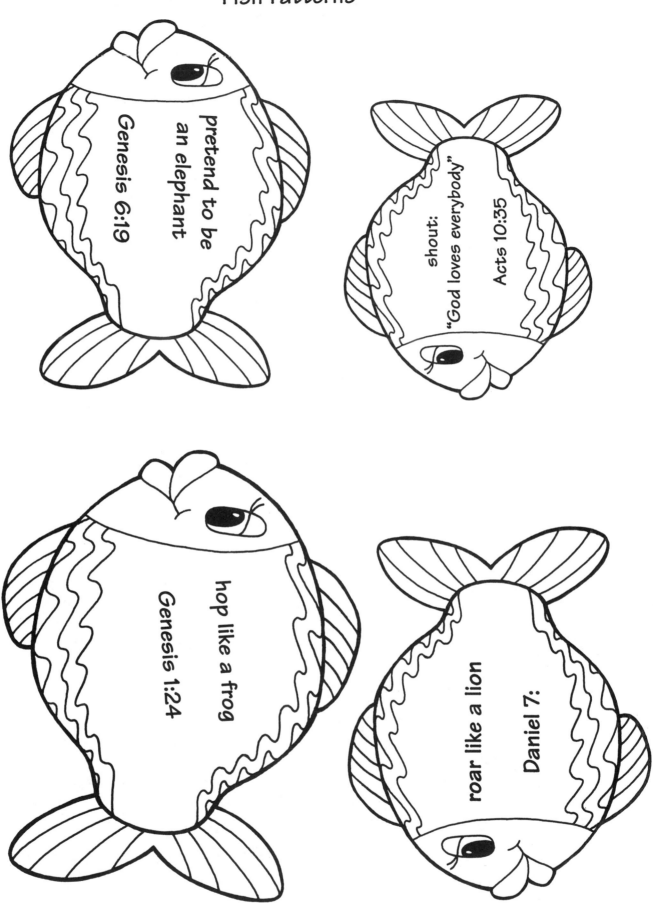

pretend to be
an elephant

Genesis 6:19

shout:
"God loves everybody"
Acts 10:35

hop like a frog
Genesis 1:24

roar like a lion
Daniel 7:

Fish Patterns

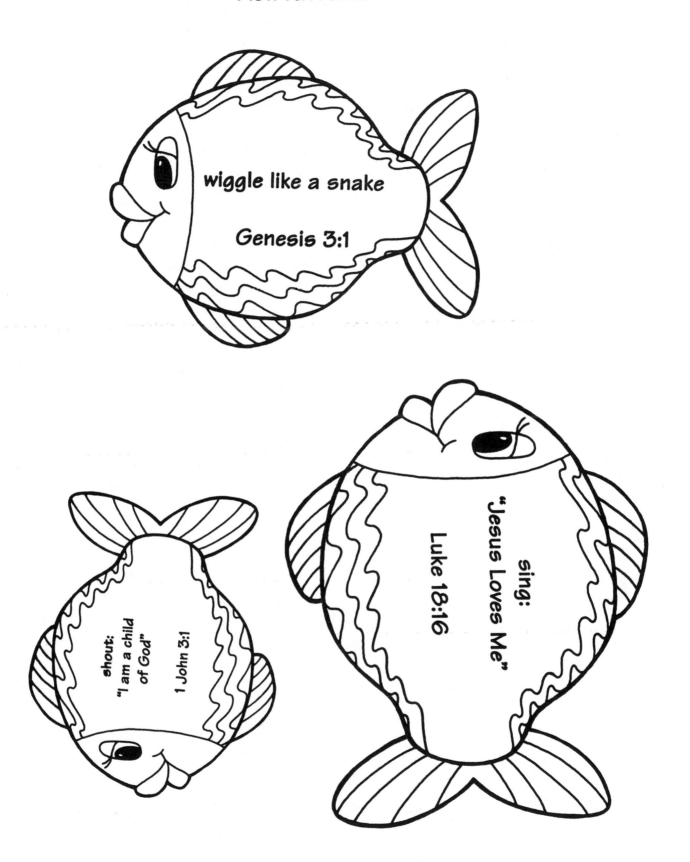

wiggle like a snake

Genesis 3:1

shout:
"I am a child of God"

1 John 3:1

sing:
"Jesus Loves Me"

Luke 18:16

Fish Patterns

jump up and
down three times

Psalm 25:1

tell someone
next to you:
"Jesus loves you,
I love you too."

John 12:34

smile a big smile

Proverbs 15:13

tell someone
next to you:
"Jesus loves you,
I love you too."

John 12:34

Fish Patterns

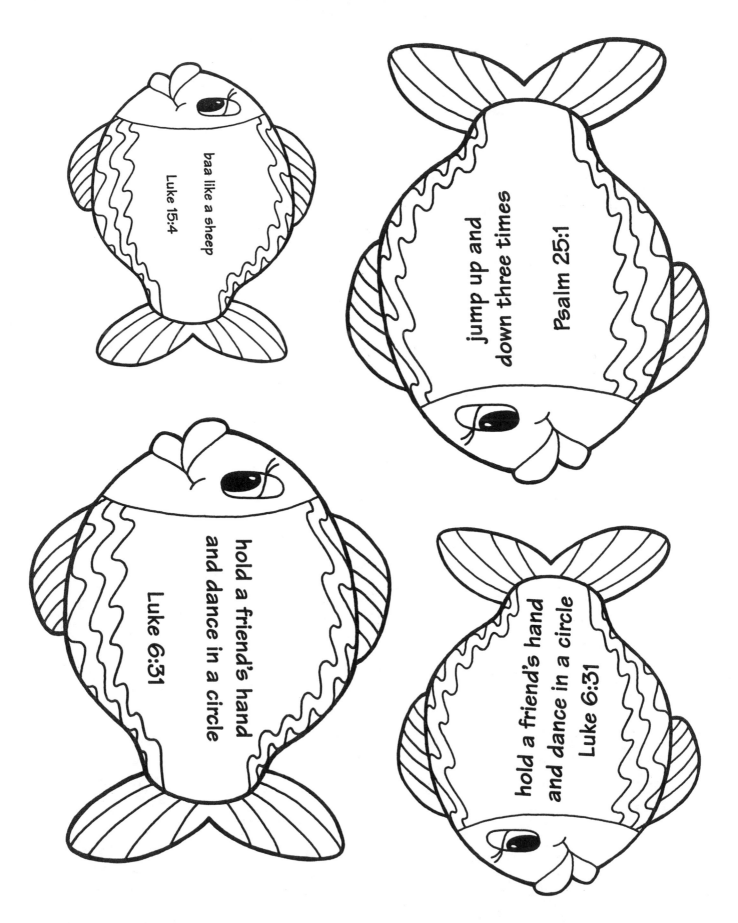

baa like a sheep

Luke 15:4

jump up and
down three times

Psalm 25:1

hold a friend's hand
and dance in a circle

Luke 6:31

hold a friend's hand
and dance in a circle

Luke 6:31

Fish Patterns

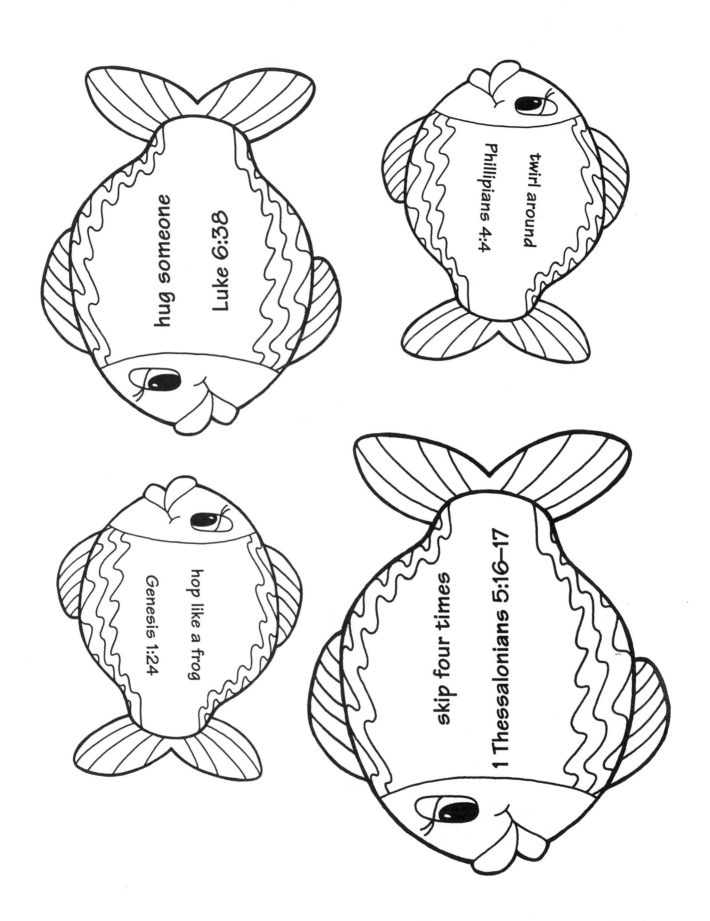

hug someone

Luke 6:38

twirl around

Phillipians 4:4

hop like a frog

Genesis 1:24

skip four times

1 Thessalonians 5:16-17

Fish Patterns

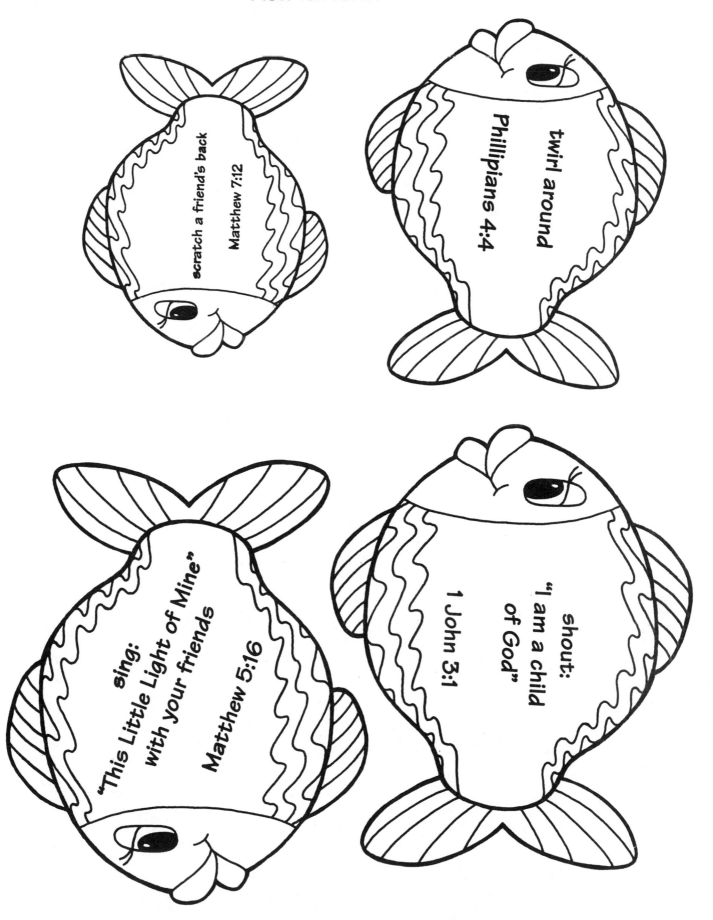

scratch a friend's back

Matthew 7:12

twirl around

Phillipians 4:4

sing:
"This Little Light of Mine"
with your friends

Matthew 5:16

shout:
"I am a child
of God"

1 John 3:1

Fish Patterns

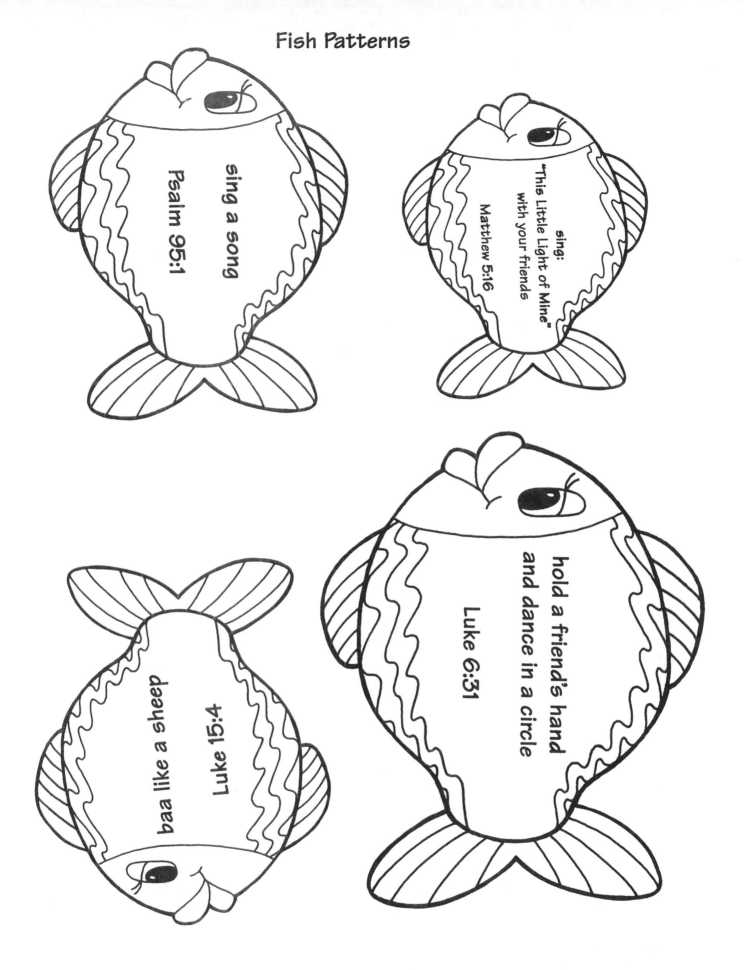

sing a song
Psalm 95:1

sing:
"This Little Light of Mine"
with your friends
Matthew 5:16

hold a friend's hand
and dance in a circle
Luke 6:31

baa like a sheep
Luke 15:4

Bible Picture Dominoes

All ages

Match the pictures end to end to reinforce Bible stories,
their lessons, and where to find them in the Bible.

What you need:

tagboard, scissors, clear contact paper, color crayons or markers.
Teacher Reference Cards found on pages 51-52.

What you do:

- Color domino cards (pages 53-64, Old Testament Domino Cards - pages 65-72, New Testament Domino Cards) if desired. Be sure to color identical pictures alike.
- Cut out and mount onto tagboard or heavy cardstock paper. Laminate with clear contact paper.
- Spread cards face down on floor or large table surface. This is the "draw" pile. Each player chooses five cards. The person with a double picture goes first. If no one has a double picture, players may take turns until one is drawn from the draw pile or players can just choose someone to play first.
- The first player lays down a Bible Picture Domino card, Play continues in a clockwise direction. The next player must match the picture of the card on the table and lay that picture end to end with the picture already in play.

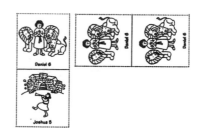

- If the player holds a double picture that matches one on the playing surface, lay it crosswise to form a three-way option for the next player.

- If a player is not holding a card that matches the one on the playing surface the player must draw another Bible Picture Domino card until they draw one that matches. It is then laid down and play moves on. Play continues until all cards have been drawn from the draw pile. The player with the fewest Bible Picture Dominoes in their hand, when all possible cards have been played, is the winner.

Variations of the game:

- To challenge children to increase their knowledge, before they can lay their dominoes down to match a picture, they must tell what Bible story is. *Example—the ark;* a child must be able to tell that the ark represents the story of the flood, when God flooded the earth and told Noah to build an ark to save the animals and his family. Then they may lay down their domino.

- To help Bible learning, children must find the book in the Bible in which the story is found before playing their domino. (Note, Bible reference is listed on each card.)

- Meaning of story—God's message to us.

- Domino cards are in sets of sixty—Old Testament (pages 53-62) and New Testament (pages 63-72). You may choose to use together or separately.

All ages, 1–8 players

Use the guide below to help guide the players through this domino game.
Look at Variations of Games to see how these cards
can be used to enhance learning.

Teacher Reference Old Testament Domino Cards

Exodus 12 – The Exodus (Moses parting the Red Sea)
God helped Moses and his people to the promised land because Moses trusted and believed in God.

Genesis 6 – Noah (ark with rainbow)
God became angry with the wickedness of the people and flooded the earth. However, God promised never to flood the earth again and the rainbow is God's covenant to for that promise.

Daniel 6 – Daniel in the lion's den
Daniel kept praying to God, even when it was against the law to pray. God remained faithful to Daniel by keeping the lions' mouths closed.

Jonah 2 – Jonah (Jonah inside of the big fish)
Even though Jonah did not obey God, God, in His mercy, still took care of Jonah inside of the fish.

Joshua 5 – The Fall of Jericho (trumpet being played with Jericho tumbling)
God helped Joshua, a faithful servant, crumble the city of Jericho.

Genesis 1 – Creation (a world in God's hand with sunbursts shooting out from it)
Our world, and all that is in it, was created by God.

1 Samuel 17 – David and Goliath
David trusted God and knew He would help him defeat the giant.

Numbers 21 – The Bronze Snake
One of God's ways to show the people of Israel His power and that He truly is God.

Luke 18 – The Rich Man (A camel trying to squeeze through the eye of a needle)
Jesus teaches that God must be first in your life. You must love God with your whole heart and put nothing in your life before him.

Luke 14 – Jesus Walking on Water (Jesus walking to boat in the distance)
To show He truly was the Son of God He walked on water.

Luke 19 – Zacchaeus (man in a tree watching Jesus as he appraoched
Jesus shows, by example, that He came to help man find God in their hearts, To show that all men can be saved and how wonderful it is when someone finds salvation in the Lord.

Luke 5 – Jesus Heals a Paralyzed Man (man being lowered through roof)
Through the faith of friends, Jesus heals a man. Lift people you love to God in prayer. Your faith is important.

Luke 10 – The Good Samaritan (one man kneeling by another man on the road, with a donkey standing nearby)
We should assist all people who need help. God works through us to show His love.

Luke 15 – The Lost Sheep (shepherd carrying sheep)
God keeps looking for all people to come to Him. When a person repents and is "found" (asks Jesus into their heart) God rejoices in heaven just like the shepherd when he found his lost sheep.

Matthew 14 – Jesus Feeds Five Thousand (Jesus holding two baskets, two fish, and five loaves of bread)
In the miracle of feeding so many people with so little food, Jesus shows he truly is the Son of God.

Matthew 28 – The Resurrection (an empty tomb with stone rolled away)
We are saved people through Christ Jesus. By raising from the dead, Jesus has given all who believe in Him everlasting life in God our Father.

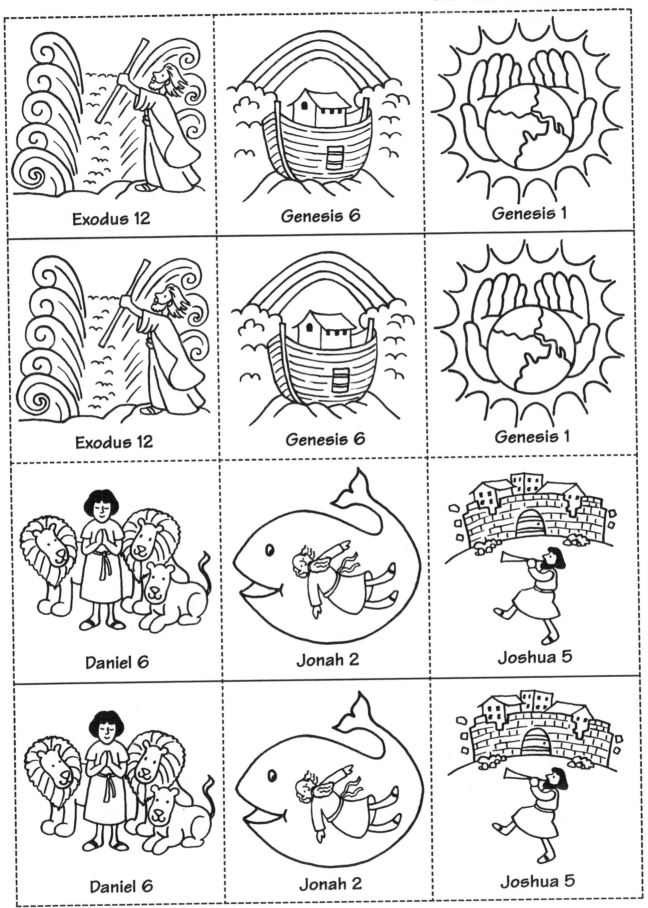

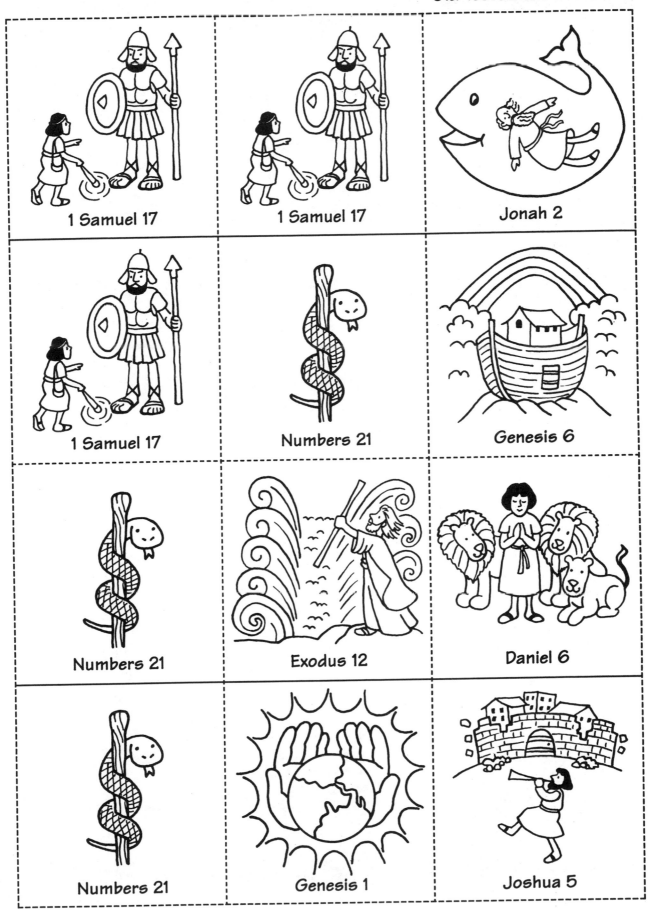

1 Samuel 17

1 Samuel 17

Jonah 2

1 Samuel 17

Numbers 21

Genesis 6

Numbers 21

Exodus 12

Daniel 6

Numbers 21

Genesis 1

Joshua 5

Genesis 1

Jonah 2

Genesis 6

Numbers 21

Daniel 6

Joshua 5

Exodus 12

1 Samuel 17

Jonah 2

Numbers 21

Joshua 5

Daniel 6

Exodus 12

Genesis 6

Genesis 1

Daniel 6

Joshua 5

Joshua 5

Jonah 2

Numbers 21

1 Samuel 17

Genesis 1

Exodus 12

Genesis 6

Genesis 6

Joshua 5

Exodus 12

Daniel 6

1 Samuel 17

Genesis 1

Jonah 2

Numbers 21

Genesis 6

Joshua 5

Exodus 12

Daniel 6

Jonah 2

Numbers 21

Genesis 1

Daniel 6

Daniel 6

1 Samuel 17

1 Samuel 17

Exodus 12

Joshua 5

Exodus 12

Daniel 6

Genesis 6

Exodus 12

Numbers 21

1 Samuel 17

Genesis 1

Exodus 12

Genesis 6

Joshua 5

1 Samuel 17

Exodus 12

1 Samuel 17

Daniel 6

Jonah 2

Jonah 2 | Daniel 6 | Numbers 21

Numbers 21 | Joshua 5 | Jonah 2

Joshua 5 | Genesis 1 | Jonah 2

Daniel 6 | Numbers 21 | Genesis 6

Numbers 21

1 Samuel 17

Genesis 6

Daniel 6

Jonah 2

Joshua 5

Exodus 12

Genesis 1

Daniel 6

Jonah 2

Exodus 12

Genesis 1

Genesis 6	Joshua 5	1 Samuel 17
Genesis 1	Jonah 2	Genesis 1
Daniel 6	Genesis 6	Genesis 1
Numbers 21	1 Samuel 17	Daniel 6

Luke 18

Matthew 14

Matthew 28

Luke 18

Matthew 14

Matthew 28

Luke 19

Luke 5

Luke 10

Luke 19

Luke 5

Luke 10

Luke 15

Luke 15

Luke 5

Luke 15

Luke 18

Luke 10

Luke 14

Luke 10

Matthew 28

Luke 14

Luke 19

Luke 10

Luke 15

Luke 5

Matthew 14

Matthew 14

Luke 19

Luke 10

Matthew 28

Luke 18

Luke 5

Matthew 14

Matthew 28

Luke 18

Luke 10

Luke 18

Matthew 14

Luke 19

Luke 10

Matthew 14

Matthew 14

Matthew 28

Luke 15

Luke 15

Luke 5

Luke 10

Matthew 14   Luke 5   Luke 18

Luke 18   Matthew 14   Luke 15

Luke 5   Matthew 28   Matthew 14

Matthew 14   Luke 10   Luke 5

Luke 10

Luke 5

Luke 19

Luke 14

Luke 14

Luke 14

Matthew 28

Luke 14

Luke 14

Matthew 28

Luke 15

Luke 19

Luke 10

Matthew 28

Luke 18

Matthew 14

Luke 19

Luke 15

Luke 18

Luke 5

Luke 15

Luke 5

Luke 15

Matthew 28

Luke 18

Luke 14

Luke 5

Matthew 28

Luke 19

Luke 14

Matthew 14

Luke 10

Matthew 14

Luke 15

Luke 5

Luke 18

With this spinner game, children learn where to locate books of the Bible as they try to beat the clock. This game includes a New Testament Spinner Game (page 74), an Old Testament Spinner Game (page 75), and a Bible Book Blank Spinner pattern so you can create your own games.

You will need:
paper clip
pencil
plastic lid
brass fastener
timer
Bible—preferably one for each player
tagboard
scissors

What you do:

- Copy and mount the wheel onto tagboard. Cut a spinner out of a plastic lid, or use a paper clip with a pencil held in the center of it for the spinner. Attach the plastic spinner with a brass fastener.
- The game can be played individually or as teams. The first player gets ready to spin and the timer is set. The player then has a designated amount of time to spin, look up the verse in the Bible, and to read the verse to the rest of the players. This needs to be done within the allocated time. You know the players best—allow enough time for them to be successful yet still be challenged. As they learn how to locate the books of the Bible, decrease the time limit.

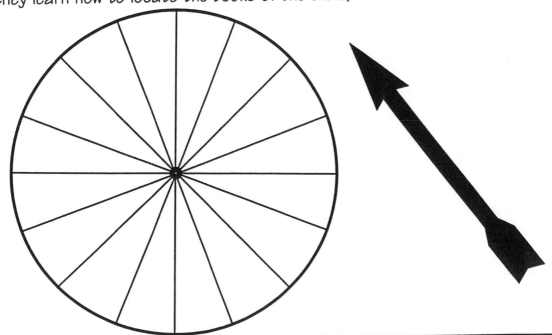

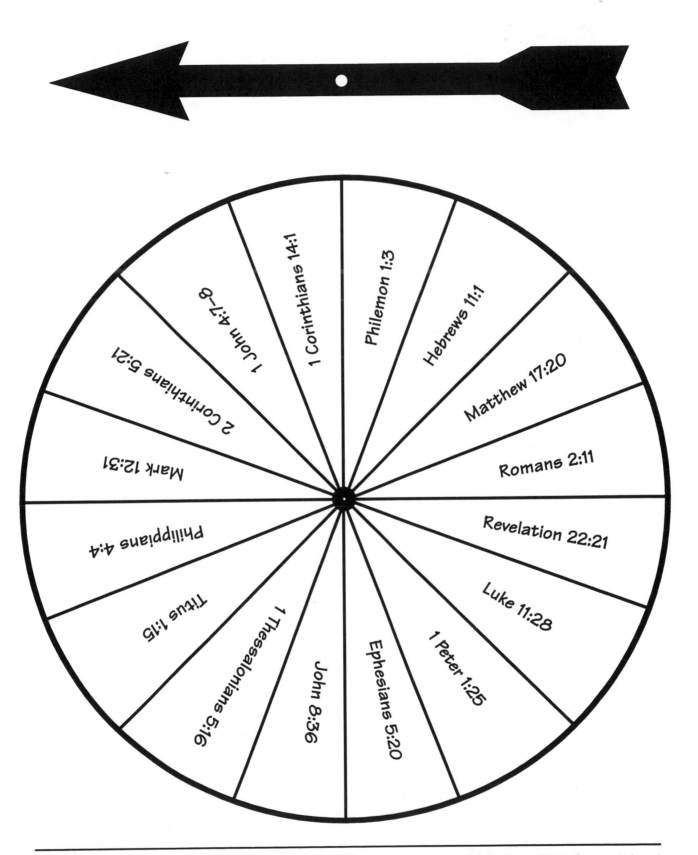

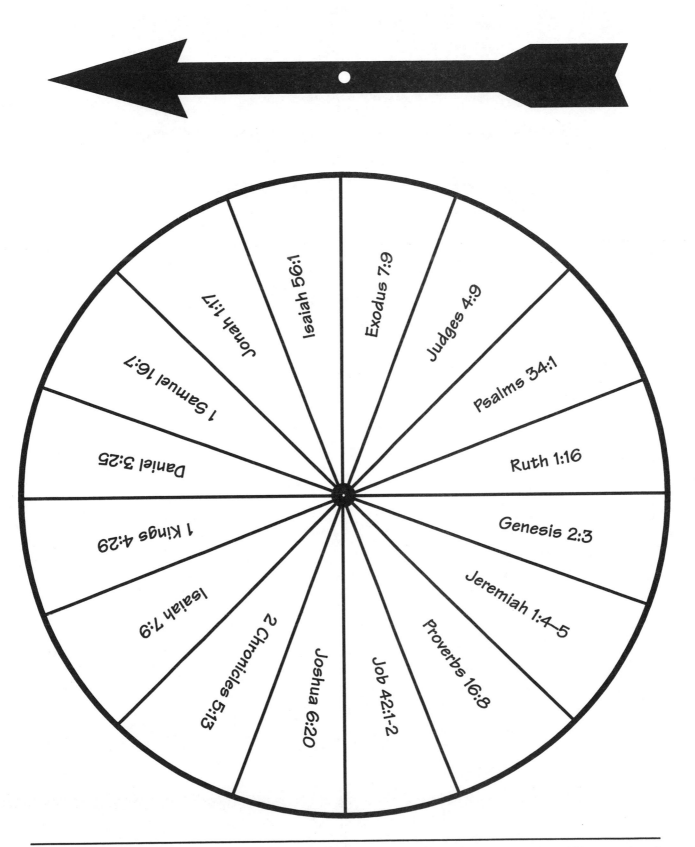

Bible Book Spinner Pattern

Make your own spinner game.
Use it to reinforce memory work for specific verses,
to reinforce your lesson, or to help children learn all the books of the Bible.

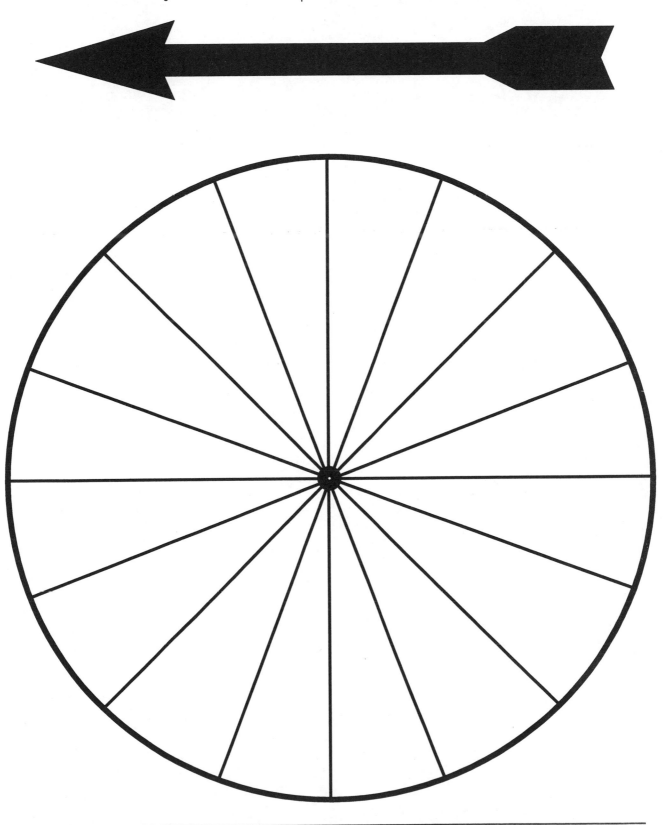

—————— Ten Commandments Game ——————

A game designed to reinforce the lessons of the Ten Commandments.
2–6 players

Scripture: Exodus 1–20

You will need:
markers for game board

What you do:
- Cut out or copy the game board (pages 78-79). Mount on a file folder.
- Copy game cards onto construction paper. Cut out the game cards, shuffle, and place on the game board.
- Copy and cut out six sets of the Ten Commandment tablets.
- Cut out the answer key and fold in half inside to make an answer booklet. (Note—each playing card is numbered for easy reference to the answer key.)
- Attach a large envelope to the folder for storage of game cards.

To play the game:
- Count out one set of Ten Commandment cards for each person playing.
- Players place markers on "start" and collect first and second commandment tablets from their sets. Place them in front of each player.
- The first player draws a game card and reads the question out loud. If he/she knows the answer, the player must follow the directions on the card. If the player does not know the answer, the player's turn is over and the game card is placed in the discard pile. If the player answers correctly, follow the directions on the card and advance on the game board. The players must also follow the directions on the game board squares.
- "You are a child of God" card is a free card. A player may collect one commandment that he/she needs from the commandment pile when this card is drawn.
- Children can take turns looking up answers in the answer book, or one person can be designated to that position, or an adult may choose to have the answer book.
- Play continues until someone reaches Moses at the end of the game board. If a player has collected all Ten Commandments, he/she is the winner. If not, play continues until one person gets to Moses with all Ten Commandments. If no player gets all Ten Commandments, the child with the most commandments wins.

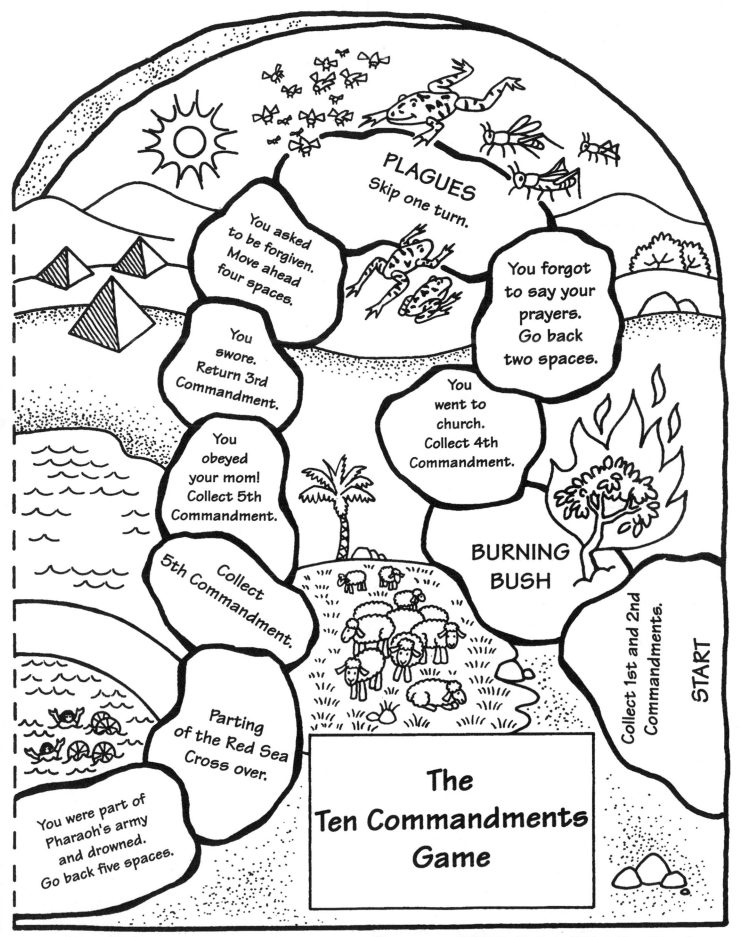

PLAGUES
Skip one turn.

You asked to be forgiven. Move ahead four spaces.

You forgot to say your prayers. Go back two spaces.

You swore. Return 3rd Commandment.

You went to church. Collect 4th Commandment.

You obeyed your mom! Collect 5th Commandment.

BURNING BUSH

Collect 5th Commandment.

Collect 1st and 2nd Commandments.

START

Parting of the Red Sea Cross over.

You were part of Pharaoh's army and drowned. Go back five spaces.

The Ten Commandments Game

Ten Commandments Answer Key

Ten Commandments Answer Key

1. You shall have no other gods before me.
2. You shall not make for yourself an idol.
3. You shall not misuse the name of the Lord your God.
4. Remember the Sabbath day by keeping it holy.
5. Honor your father and your mother.
6. You shall not murder.
7. You shall not commit adultery.
8. You shall not steal.
9. You shall not give false testimony against your neighbor.
10. You shall not covet.
11. You shall have no other gods before me.

Ten Commandments Answer Key

12. You shall not make for yourself an idol.
13. You shall not misuse the name of the Lord your God.
14. Remember the Sabbath day by keeping it holy.
15. Honor your father and your mother.
16. You shall not murder.
17. You shall not commit adultery.
18. You shall not steal.
19. You shall not give false testimony against your neighbor.
20. You shall not covet.
21. Moses
22. Mount Sinai
23. 1st Commandment – worship false god
24. Golden calf

Ten Commandments Answer Key

25. Blood, frogs, gnats, flies, livestock, boils, hail, locusts, darkness, and death of firstborn
26. Burning bush
27. Turned into a snake.
28. Aaron
29. So God would pass over their homes and not kill the firstborn.
30. Put blood from a lamb on the top and sides of door frames.
31. A pillar of clouds by day, a pillar of fire by night.
32. They drowned.
33. The Red Sea
34. The Ten Commandments
35. 1st Commandment
36. 10th Commandment

Ten Commandments Answer Key

37. 8th Commandment
38. His heart
39. The Passover. God killed the first-born except those with blood on their door.
40. Yes
41. Water
42. Egypt
43. Straw
44. Moses
45. Placed in a basket and set in the river, found by Pharaoh's daughter.
46. The Nile
47. The Red Sea parted.
48. God
49. Exodus
50. Exodus

Ten Commandments Tablet Cards

Make one set of cards for each player.

1st Commandment
You shall have no other gods before me.

2nd Commandment
You shall not make for yourself an idol.

3rd Commandment
You shall not misuse the name of the Lord your God.

4th Commandment
Remember the Sabbath day by keeping it holy.

5th Commandment
Honor your father and your mother.

6th Commandment
You shall not murder.

7th Commandment
You shall not commit adultery.

8th Commandment
You shall not steal.

9th Commandment
You shall not give false testimony against your neighbor.

10th Commandment
You shall not covet.

Ten Commandments Playing Cards
Copy on to construction paper and cut apart.

What is the 1st Commandment? Collect it. Move ahead 1 space. **1**	What is the 2nd commandment? Collect it. Move ahead 1 space. **2**	What is the 3rd Commandment? Collect it. Move ahead 2 spaces. **3**
What is the 4th Commandment? Collect it. Move ahead 2 spaces. **4**	What is the 5th Commandment? Collect it. Move ahead 2 spaces. **5**	What is the 6th Commandment? Collect it. Move ahead 3 spaces. **6**
What is the 7th Commandment? Collect it. Move ahead 1 space. **7**	What is the 8th commandment? Collect it. Move ahead 2 spaces. **8**	What is the 9th Commandment? Collect it. Move ahead 2 spaces. **9**
What is the 10th Commandment? Collect it. Move ahead 2 spaces. **10**	What is the 1st Commandment? Collect it. Move ahead 1 space. **11**	What is the 2nd commandment? Collect it. Move ahead 1 space. **12**
What is the 3rd Commandment? Collect it. Move ahead 2 spaces. **13**	What is the 4th Commandment? Collect it. Move ahead 2 spaces. **14**	What is the 5th Commandment? Collect it. Move ahead 2 spaces. **15**
What is the 6th Commandment? Collect it. Move ahead 3 spaces. **16**	What is the 7th Commandment? Collect it. Move ahead 1 space. **17**	What is the 8th commandment? Collect it. Move ahead 2 spaces. **18**

Ten Commandments Playing Cards
Copy on to construction paper and cut apart.

What is the 9th Commandment? Collect it. Move ahead 2 spaces. 19	What is the 10th Commandment? Collect it. Move ahead 1 space. 20	Who brought the Commandments down from the mountain? Move ahead 1 space 21
What mountain did Moses receive the commandments on? Move ahead 3 spaces 22	What Commandment did Moses' people break when they grew tired of waiting for him to return? Move ahead 1 space 23	What did Moses' people make to worship that was wrong? Move ahead 2 spaces. 24
God sent ten plagues onto Pharaoh— name two of them. Move ahead 2 spaces 25	What did God talk through to speak to Moses while he was tending sheep? Move ahead 3 spaces 26	What happened to Moses' staff when God told him to throw it on the ground? Move ahead 1 space 27
Who did God send into the desert to meet Moses? Move ahead 2 spaces 28	Why did God's people put lamb's blood on the top and sides of their door frames? Move ahead 3 spaces 29	What did God instruct Moses to tell his people to do so that death of the firstborn would not touch them? Move ahead 2 spaces 30
How did God guide Moses and his people as they fled Egypt? Move ahead 1 space 31	What happened to Pharaoh's army when they followed Moses into the Red Sea? Move ahead 2 spaces 32	What was the name of the sea Moses had to cross to flee from Egypt? Go to Parting of the Red Sea 33
What did Moses bring down from Mt. Sinai? Move ahead 1 space 34	You made money more important than God. What Commandment did you break? Go to Plagues 35	You really want your best friend's bike. What Commandment refers to this? Move ahead 2 spaces 36

Ten Commandment Playing Cards
Copy on to construction paper and cut apart.

You stole candy from the store. What Commandment did you break? Go to Burning Bush 37	What did Pharaoh harden against God? Move ahead 1 space 38	What happened that made Pharaoh tell Moses to leave Egypt and worship his God? Move ahead 3 spaces 39
Did Pharaoh and his army follow Moses after he let them go? Move ahead 2 spaces 40	What came out of the rock of Horeb when Moses struck it with his staff as God instructed? Move ahead 3 spaces 41	What land did God help Moses and his people leave? Move ahead 2 spaces 42
Pharaoh made the Israelites make bricks without supplying them with what? Move ahead 3 spaces 43	Who did God choose to help lead the Israelites out of Egypt? Move ahead 2 spaces 44	What happened to Moses when he was a baby? Move ahead 2 spaces 45
What river was Moses put into as a baby? Move ahead 2 spaces 46	When Moses held his staff over the Red Sea, what happened? Move ahead 1 space 47	Who protected Moses and the Israelites against Pharaoh? Move ahead 2 spaces 48
What book in the Bible contains the Ten Commandments? Move ahead 3 spaces 49	Moses' life and leaving Egypt is found in what book of the Bible? Move ahead 2 spaces 50	You are a child of God. Collect one Commandment
You are a child of God. Collect one Commandment	You are a child of God. Collect one Commandment	You are a child of God. Collect one Commandment

A Bible Trivia Game

This game reinforces Bible knowledge. As children play Bible Baseball, and answers are given, children will discover things they did not know about the Bible.

You know the level of knowledge the children have who are playing the game so use discretion when using the question book so that success can be obtained. The question book contains both an early elementary section with simpler, basic questions, and an advanced elementary section that has more difficult questions.

Set-up Game Board:
- Cut out and mount playing field onto a folder. You may wish to color the playing field gameboard. This will also become the storage unit when the game is not being used. Attach a large envelope to the outside of the folder to hold the playing pieces and dice.

The Question Booklet:
- Cut out question pages on solid line and fold on the dotted line. Put them together and staple on the fold to form your booklet.

Game Pieces:
- Copy each game piece, color each of the stands a different color and mount on cardboard. You make as many players as you need. Children can share players when a team is up to bat or you can have two separate teams of players.

You will need:
- Dice, file folder, large envelope, pencil, and cardboard.

Scorecard
- Make several copies of the scorecard and keep with game in the folder. Write in team name.
- Use top half of box to keep track of runs scoredthat inning. Put the total runs scored per inning in the bottom box.

To play the game:
- Have the children divide into two baseball teams and give their team a name. Decide who will be up to bat first. The first batter puts his marker on home plate and then rolls the dice. 1 = single, 2 = double, 3 = triple, 4 = homerun, 5 = foul ball (roll again), and 6 = fly out (next batter up).

- A question is then asked of the first batter. It is not necessary to read questions in order. Skim through and find one appropriate for the player answering the question. Each player gets three chances (strikes) to answer the question correctly. If the child answers correctly, they may move their marker to appropriate base. If the question is not answered correctly that player is out. and the next player comes up to bat. If there are already players on base when another question is answered correctly, those players move the same amount of bases as the player up to bat. For example: is the player up to bat gets a single, all the players on base move up one base. If the player up to bat gets a double, all the players on base move up two bases.

- If a player rolls a 6, or cannot answer the question correctly after three attempts, they are out. Mark an out box on the scorecard for that inning. When a team has three outs the other team comes up to bat.

- Length of game can be by the number of innings or by length of time. If you have fifteen minutes, use that as the time limit and play as many innings as possible.

- Highest scoring team at the end of the game is the winner.

Bible Baseball Gameboard Markers

Copy and mount on cardboard—cut on dotted line cut on solid line to fit on stand.

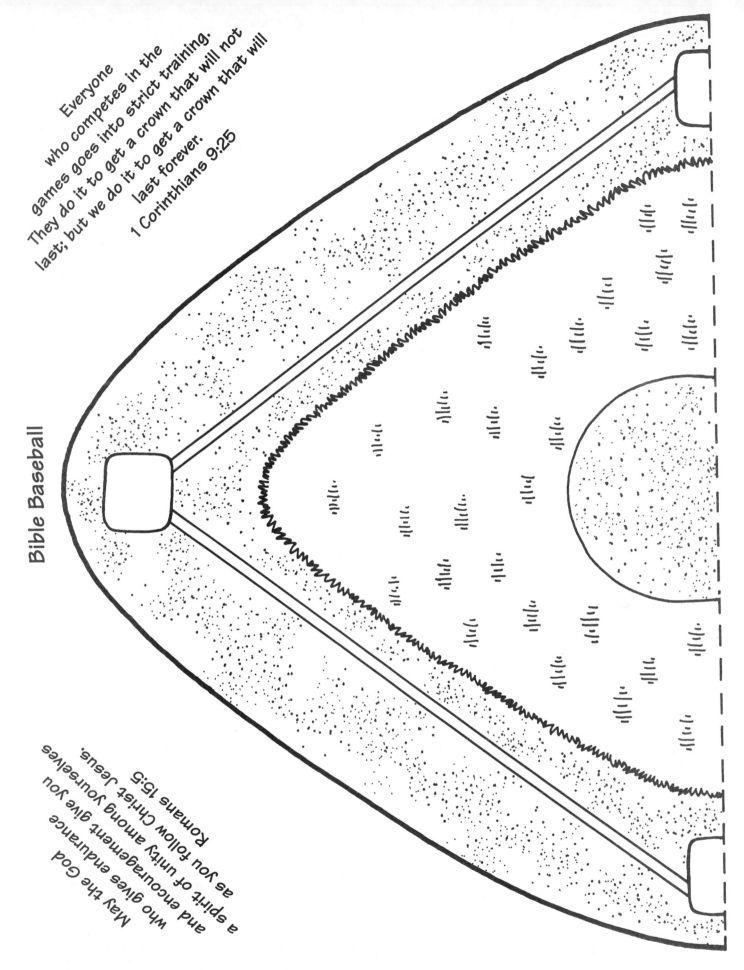

Bible Baseball

Everyone who competes in the games goes into strict training. They do it to get a crown that will not last; but we do it to get a crown that will last forever.
1 Corinthians 9:25

May the God who gives endurance and encouragement give you a spirit of unity among yourselves as you follow Christ Jesus.
Romans 15:5

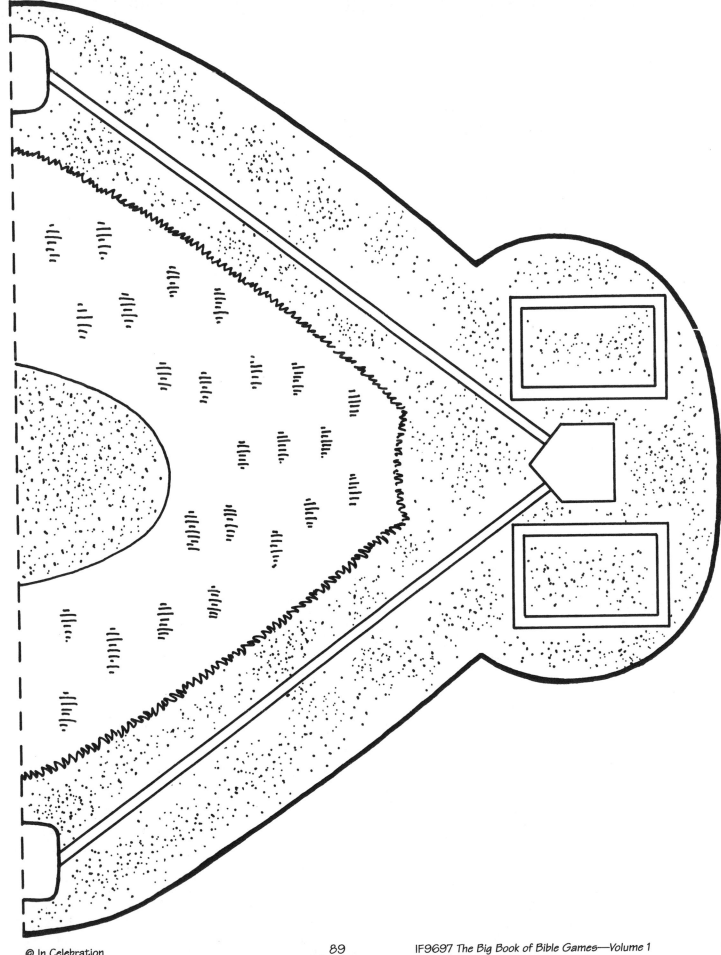

Bible Baseball Scorecards

TEAM	1	OUTS	2	OUTS	3	OUTS	4	OUTS	5	OUTS	6	OUTS	7	OUTS	8	OUTS	9	OUTS	TOTAL
Total for Inning																			
Total for Inning																			

TEAM	1	OUTS	2	OUTS	3	OUTS	4	OUTS	5	OUTS	6	OUTS	7	OUTS	8	OUTS	9	OUTS	TOTAL
Total for Inning																			
Total for Inning																			

Bible Trivia
Questions

BIBLE
BASEBALL

Q: Why did Zacchaeus climb a tree?
A: To see Jesus.

Q: What was Jesus doing in the storm when the apostles were so frightened?
A: Sleeping.

Q: Who did an angel help out of prison?
A: Peter.

Q: "God is our refuge and _____, a very present help in trouble." (Psalms 46:1)
A: Strength.

Q: How many plagues did God send upon the Egyptians?
A: Ten.

Q: What does Jesus tell us to do to our enemies?
A: Love them.

Q: How many Beatitudes did Jesus give in Matthew 5?
A: Eight

27

Rules of the Game

- Have children form two teams (they can select team names for cheering and scoring purposes)

- Each player gets three chances (strikes) to answer a question.

- After three outs play moves to the next team.

- Roll of the dice:

  1 = single   4 = homerun
  2 = double   5 = foul ball (roll again)
  3 = triple   6 = fly out, next batter up

- Length of game should be determined before you start playing the game. Time or number of innings can be your guide.

2

Early
Elementary
Questions

3

Q: What was the place of worship for god's people before the temple?

A: Tabernacle.

Q: Who was found in a basket by Pharaoh's daughter?

A: Moses.

Q: Who were John the Baptist's parents?

A: Elisabeth and Zacharias.

Q: What three friends of Daniel were cast into the fiery furnace?

A: Shadrach, Meshach, and Abednego.

Q: What is the last book in the Old Testament?

A: Malachi.

Q: Name Six of the twelve apostles.

A: Peter, Andrew, James, John, Philip, Matthew, Bartholomew, Thomas, James the son of Alphueus, Thaddaeus, Simon of Zealot, and Judas.

26

Q: Ten brothers sold their younger brother into slavery. What was his name?

A: Joseph

Q: What king arrested John the Baptist and had him beheaded?

A: Herod

Q: Who was Mary and Martha's brother whom Jesus raised from the dead?

A: Lazarus

Q: You shall not misuse the _____ of the Lord your God.

A: Name

Q: How many gospel books are there?

A: Four

Q: What was the occupation of Peter, Andrew, James, and John?

A: Fisherman

Q: Who was the first woman?

A: Eve

25

Q: When you are afraid who should you trust?

A: The Lord.

Q: Jesus said, "I am the vine, you are the _____." (John 15:5)

A: Branches

Q: What did David use to kill Goliath?

A: Slingshot.

Q: What did Joseph's brothers do to him?

A: Sold him into slavery

Q: What do we read to learn about God and what he wants for us?

A: The Bible.

Q: What is The Golden Rule?

A: Do unto others as you would have them do unto you.

4

Q: What did the big fish do to Jonah after he was in his stomach for three days?
A: Spit him out.

Q: What did people wave and throw down in Jesus' path as He rode into Jerusalem on a donkey?
A: Palm branches.

Q: What did God put in the sky to show His promise to never flood the earth again?
A: A Rainbow.

Q: Who rolled away the stone at Jesus' tomb?
A: An angel.

Q: Where was Jesus when his mom and dad could not find him?
A: At the temple.

5

Q: Paul tells us to "Put on the whole _____ of God." (Ephesians 6:11)
A: Armor

Q: What tribe is known as the priestly tribe?
A: The tribe of Levi.

Q: Who helped Jesus carry the cross to Calvary?
A: Simon of Cyrene.

Q: How old was Jesus when He began His ministry?
A: Thirty.

Q: Who is the King of Kings and Lord of Lords?
A: Jesus.

Q: In what language was the New Testament originally written?
A: Greek.

24

Q: Who tempted Jesus three times?
A: The devil

Q: Where did John the Baptist baptize Jesus?
A: The Jordan River

Q: How many apostles did Jesus have?
A: Twelve

Q: Jesus tells us to "Love on _____." (John 15:12)
A: Another.

Q: How many books are in the Bible?
A: Sixty-six

Q: What apostle betrayed Jesus?
A: Judas

Q: "In the beginning God created the _____ and the _____." (Genesis 1:1)
A: Heavens, Earth.

23

Q: What did Mary lay Jesus in after He was born?
A: A manger.

Q: Who was swallowed by a big fish?
A: Jonah.

Q: How did Jesus die?
A: He hung on a cross; crucified.

Q: What was Jesus riding when He rode into Jerusalem?
A: A donkey.

Q: What did Jesus feed five-thousand people with?
A: Two fish and five loaves of bread.

Q: Who was found in a basket floating on a river when he was a baby?
A: Moses.

6

Q: Where was Jesus born?
A: Bethlehem.

Q: Who built an ark?
A: Noah.

Q: God closed the lions' mouths so they would not eat this man.
A: Daniel.

Q: Who was in the fields with their sheep when the angel said to them that a baby had been born?
A: Shepherds.

Q: God gave strength to _____ as long as he did not cut his hair?
A: Samson.

Q: Who said, "I am the light of the world."?
A: Jesus.

7

Q: What is the sword of the Spirit?
A: The Bible.

Q: Jesus said, "I am the Alpha and the Omega, the beginning and the _____.
A: End.

Q: Who rolled the stone away from Jesus' tomb?
A: An angel.

Q: In what book(s) of the Bible are the Ten Commandments found?
A: Exodus, Deuteronomy.

Q: What boy king found a lost book when the temple was being repaired?
A: Josiah.

Q: How many books of the Bible did Peter write?
A: Two, 1 and 2 Peter.

22

Q: What happened to Lot's wife when she looked back and disobeyed God?
A: She turned into a pillar of salt.

Q: What woman had seven devils?
A: Mary Magdalene.

Q: How many years did the children of Israel wander in the wilderness?
A: Forty.

Q: Where did Jesus go with His apostles for the last supper the night before his arrest?
A: The upper room.

Q: Who appeared to Moses in a burning bush?
A: An angel of the Lord.

Q: Who did Abraham allow to choose his own land?
A: Lot.

21

Q: How many of each animal did Noah bring onto the ark?
A: Two.

Q: Who kissed Jesus in the garden of Gethsemane to tell the soldiers this was who they should take away?
A: Judas.

Q: Jesus told Peter that he would deny knowing him three times before the _____ crowed.
A: Cock.

Q: When Jesus was baptized, what came down near his head?
A: A dove.

Q: What city crumbled when a trumpet was blasted?
A: Jericho

Q: Who created the heavens and the earth?

8

Q: Jesus healed ten men with leprosy, how many said thank you?
A: One.

Q: Jesus got very angry when he saw people selling things in the temple. What did he do to them?
A: Threw them out.

Q: This boy killed Goliath with his slingshot.
A: David.

Q: What did God do so that Daniel would not get eaten by the lions?
A: Closed their mouths.

Q: What part of the Bible caovers the time after Jesus was born?
A: The New Testament.

Q: Who died on the cross?
A: Jesus.

9

Q: From what direction did the wisemen come to see Jesus?
A: The East.

Q: Who wrote most of the Psalms?
A: David.

Q: What king built the first temple?
A: Solomon.

Q: Who was Abraham's wife?
A: Sarah.

Q: When Jesus was on the cross He said. "Father, _____ them, for they know not what they do." (Luke 23:34)
A: Forgive.

Q: How long did it rain when Noah was in the ark?
A: Forty days and forty nights.

Q: What man from the Old Testament is known for his patience?
A: Job.

20

Q: Who was so strong that he killed a lion with his bare hands?

A: Samson

Q: How many people did Noah take with him into the ark?

A: Seven (his wife, his three sons, and their wives)

Q: What was placed on Christ's head before he was crucified?

A: A crown of thorns.

Q: Who was Peter's brother?

A: Andrew

Q: Who became the leader of God's people when Moses died?

A: Joshua

Q: Who was swallowed by a big fish?

A: Jonah

Q: What book of the Bible is a collection of love songs?

A: Song of Solomon.

19

Q: An angel told _____ she was chosen by God to be Jesus' mother.

A: Mary

Q: Jesus had this animal feed Elijah.

A: Ravens.

Q: How do we talk to God?

A: Through prayer.

Q: Who did God send to save the world?

A: His Son.

Q: What happened three days after Jesus was in the tomb?

A: He rose again.

10

Q: What did the wisemen follow to find baby Jesus?
A: The star.

Q: How long did it rain when Noah was in the ark?
A: Forty days and forty nights.

Q: How did Moses and his people get across the Red Sea?
A: God parted it.

Q: Who had a beautiful coat of many colors?
A: Joseph.

Q: What did people worship while Moses was on the mountain with God?
A: A golden calf.

Q: What forbidden food did Eve eat?
A: Fruit from the tree of knowledge.

11

Q: What follower of Jesus anointed His head with precious ointment? Mary, Martha, or Joanna?
A: Mary

Q: One Old Testament Commandment is "Honor your _____ and your _____." (Exodus 20:12)
A: Father, Mother

Q: Name one person Jesus raised from the dead.
A: Lazarus; the widow's son of Nain; Jairus's daughter.

Q: How many books of history are in the Old Testament?
A: Twelve.

Q: What sermon of Jesus begins with the beatitudes?
A: Sermon on the Mount.

Q: Who is the chief cornerstone of the church?
A: Jesus Christ.

18

Q: God spoke to Moses once through this.
A: A burning bush.

Q: What were on the tablets Moses brought down from the mountain?
A: The Ten Commandments.

Q: What did friends do with their paralyzed friend so Jesus might heal him?
A: Lowered him through a roof.

Q: What was Jesus doing in the boat when a big storm came up?
A: Sleeping.

Q: Who baptized Jesus?
A: John the Baptist.

Q: Who loves you all the time?
A: Jesus.

12

Q: What is the shortest verse in the bible?
A: "Jesus wept." (John 11:35)

Q: What did Jesus do to the money changers in the temple?
A: Cast or threw them out.

Q: What did Zacchaeus do to see Jesus?
A: He climbed a tree.

Q: Who spoke to Samuel in the middle of the night?
A: God.

Q: John says that "God is _____." (1 John 4:8)
A: Love.

Q: How many sons did Jacob have?
A: Twelve.

Q: Jesus even knows the number of _____ on your head?
A: Hairs.

Q: Why did Jesus die on the cross?
A: To save us from our sins.

17

Q: Who wrote 1 and 2 Samuel?
A: Samuel.

Q: Why do we observe the Lord's Supper?
A: To remember Jesus' death until he returns.

Q: What criminal was set free instead of Jesus?
A: Barabbas.

Q: In what town did Jesus grow up?
A: Nazareth.

Q: How did God lead Moses and the people to the promised land?
A: A cloud by day, and fire at night.

Q: What Roman ruler sentenced Jesus to death?
A: Pontius Pilate.

Q: What city did God tell Jonah to visit?
A: Nineveh.

13

Q: What was the name of the garden where Jesus prayed?
A: Gethsemane.

Q: Paul says that "all have _____, and fall short of the glory of God." (Romans 3:23)
A: Sinned.

Q: In what book are the beatitudes found?
A: Matthew.

Q: Who was Adam and Eve's third son?
A: Seth.

Q: Jesus called himself the bread of _____. (John 6:35)
A: Life

Q: What city did Joshua's army march around for seven days?
A: Jericho.

16

Q: Name two books of the Bible named after women.

A: *Esther, Ruth.*

Q: Name the three apostles who went to pray with Jesus in the garden.

A: *Peter, James, and John.*

Q: How many criminals were crucified along with Jesus?

A: *Two.*

Q: What promise did God make when He placed a rainbow in the sky?

A: *Never to destroy the earth again.*

Q: What does the word "gospel" mean?

A: *Good news or good tidings.*

Q: How many of each kind of animal did Noah take into the ark?

A: *Two.*

Q: Who gave us the model of the Lord's Prayer?

A: *Jesus.*

14

Q: "God created man in his own _____" (Genesis 1:27)

A: *Image*

Q: On what day was the church founded?

A: *Pentecost.*

Q: Where was Jesus when the devil tempted Him three times?

A: *In the wilderness.*

Q: Who refused to give up his riches and follow Jesus?

A: *The rich young ruler.*

Q: Who had a dream about a ladder ascending to heaven?

A: *Jacob.*

Q: Who was Isaiah referring to when he said, "For unto us a child is born, unto us a son is given; and the government shall be upon his shoulder" (Isaiah 9:6)?

A: *Jesus.*

15

Bible Story Dice Throw

2–4 players
All ages
To reinforce Bible characters and stories through this fun dice game

	Old Testament	**New Testament**
Scripture Source:	Genesis, Exodus, Daniel, 1 Samuel	Luke

What you need:

clear contact paper	scissors
cup	tagboard
tape	colored construction paper or crayons/colored markers

What you do:

- Copy and glue dice patterns onto tagboard. Cut on the bold line and fold on the dotted lines. Tape closed. (You may want to color the dice before folding into a square.). You will need five dice for each game (Old Testament and New Testament). Noah, Moses, David, Daniel, Adam & Eve, and a star are on the Old Testament Bible Story dice. The empty tomb, baby Jesus, lunch for 5000, the wisemen, John the Baptist, and a star are on the New Testament Bible Story dice. These are two separate games and cannot be used together.

- Copy the Bible Story player's markers. Each player needs a separate color. You can do this by copying the markers on different colored construction paper, or by hand coloring each set. You may want to cover with clear contact paper before cutting out. Cut out each set.

- Tear out or copy Master Bible Story Dice Throw Game Card for the game you are making (Old Testament or New Testament). Attach to tagboard or file folder and cover with clear contact paper. If using a file folder, attach an envelope to opposite side of folder for storing the game pieces. You are ready to play Bible Story Dice Throw.

Object of the game:

- Try to match as many of the same pictures on the dice as you can on each turn.

How play to play:

- Place the Master Card in the center of table where it can be easily reached by all players. Hand out a set of Bible Story Dice Throw marker pictures to each player (children may choose their own color). Show the players how all of the pictures; the master card, the player's markers and the dice are all the same,

except for the star on the dice. The star is a "wild" picture that can be used for any picture the player is trying to match.

- Everyone has a duplicate set of markers, only with different colors, that they will use on the Master Card.

- The first player puts the dice in a cup and shakes them out. The player gets three turns to roll the dice and collect as many of one picture as they can. Remember that the stars are "wild" and can be matched with any picture the player is collecting. The player then takes their marker and places it on the corresponding Master Card. *Example:* if the player has collected three Moses and one star on their three rolls, their marker would go in the Moses row under the number four. Only one marker can be placed on each square of the Master Card. If a square is already occupied the player must put their marker on the next lowest number on the Master Card. *Example:* if Moses is filled under the five and four and the player rolls five Moses, the player must put their marker on the three column, the first available square.

- Play continues until everyone has placed their markers on the Bible Story Dice throw Master Card. The players then total their scores by adding their markers together based on what column they were placed during the game. The player with the highest score wins.

New Testament Bible Story Dice Throw Player's Markers

Color each set a different color.

Player one: (color red)

Player two: (color blue)

Player three: (color green)

Player four: (color yellow)

Old Testament Bible Story Dice Throw Player's Markers

Color each set a different color.

Player one: (color red)

Player two: (color blue)

Player three: (color green)

Player four: (color yellow)

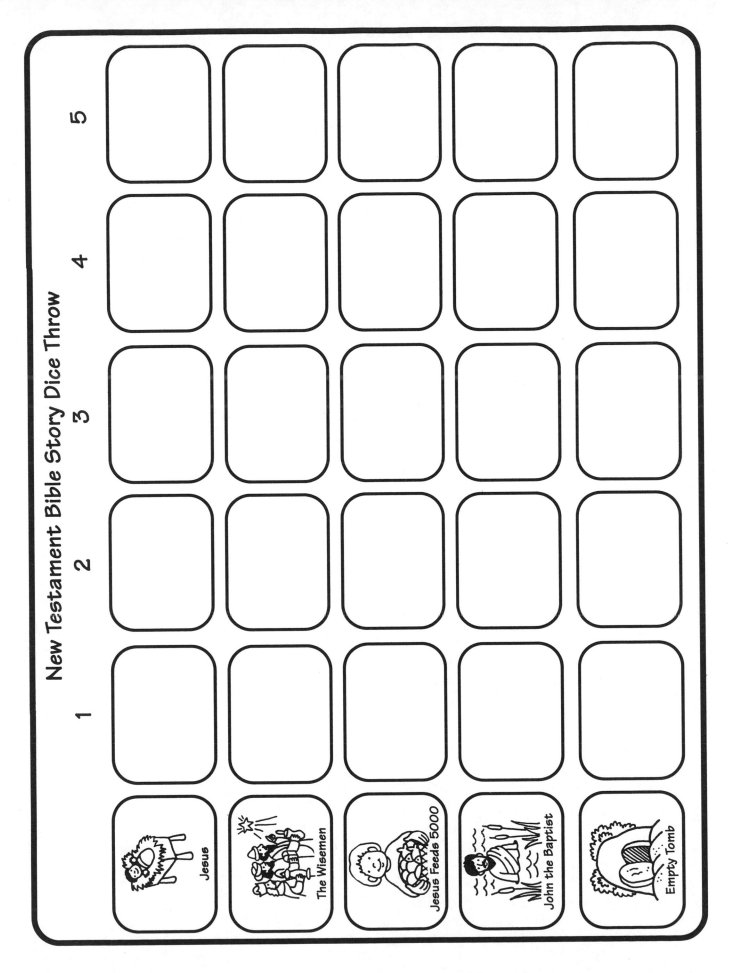

New Testament Bible Story Dice Throw

	1	2	3	4	5
Jesus					
The Wisemen					
Jesus Feeds 5000					
John the Baptist					
Empty Tomb					

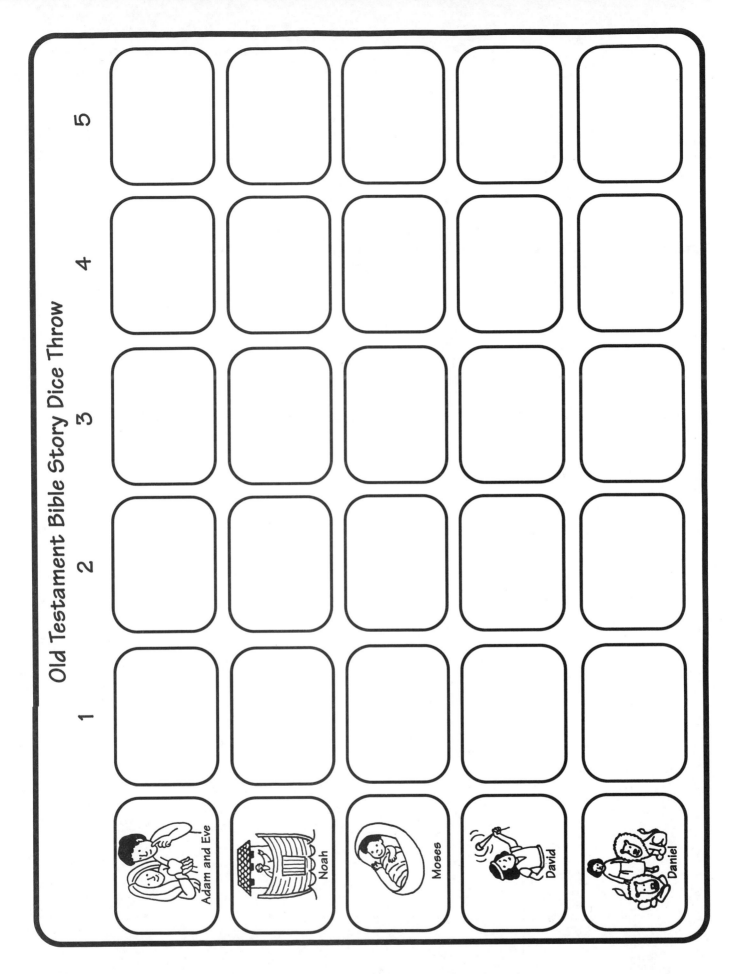

Old Testament Bible Story Dice Throw

5   4   3   2   1

Adam and Eve   Noah   Moses   David   Daniel

New Testament Dice

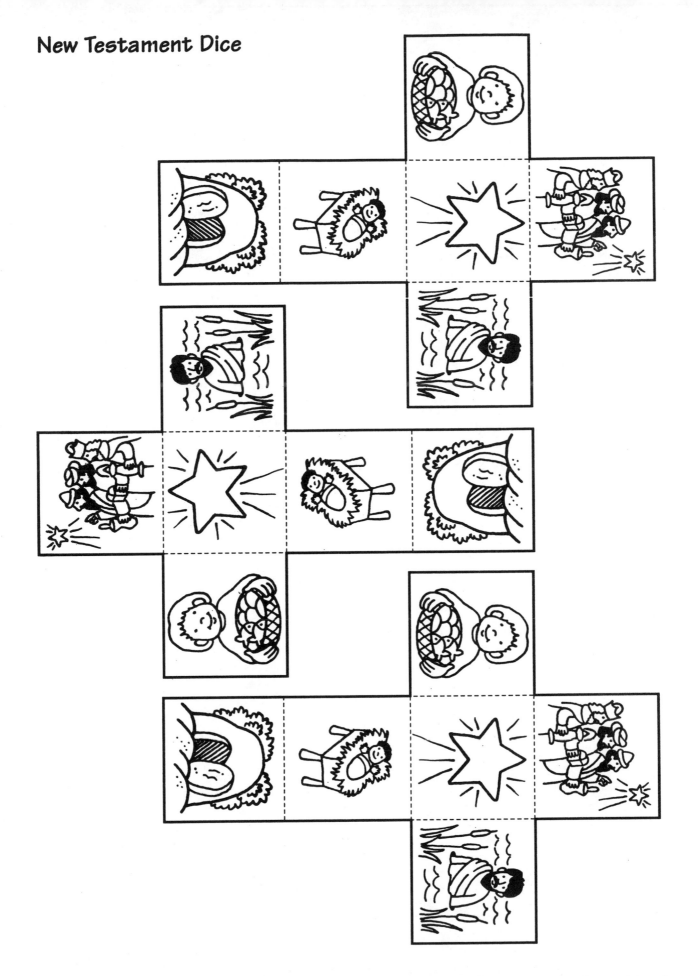

New Testament Dice

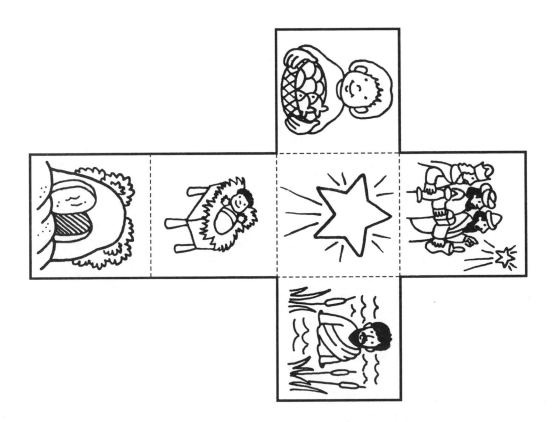

Old Testament Dice

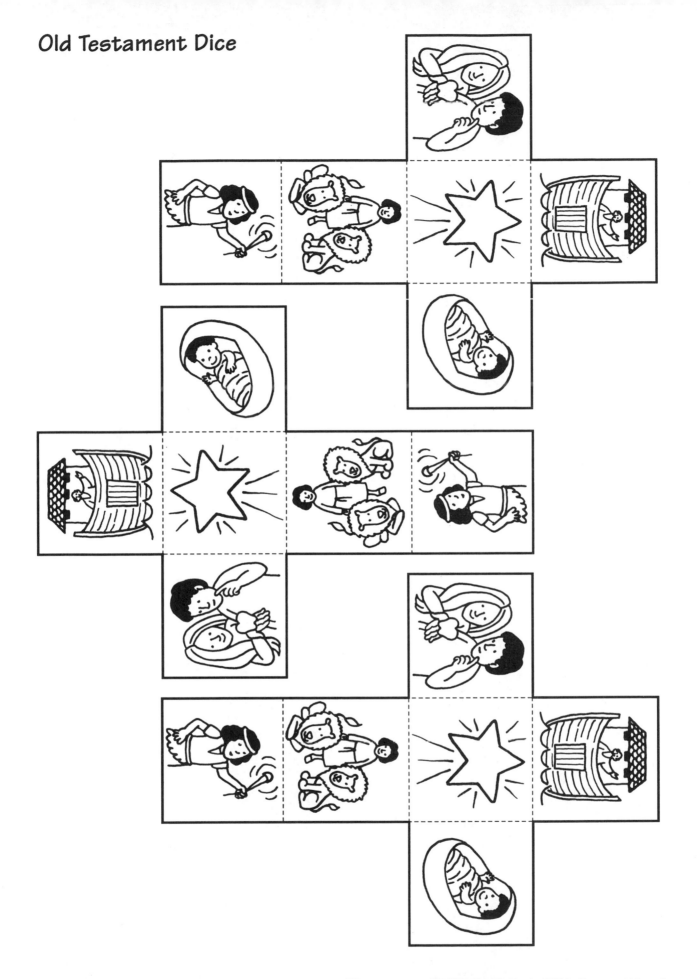

Old Testament Dice

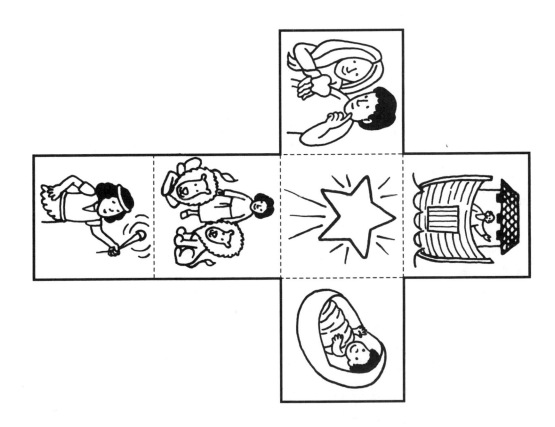

The Parable of the Lost Sheep Game

Scripture Source: Luke 15: 1–7

Jesus uses this parable to teach us how God values all of His children. He will not stop looking for those who want to repent and ask Jesus to live in their heart. God celebrates more when one person repents their sins than by having ninety-nine righteous persons who need no repentance.

In the parable of the Lost Sheep Game, children move around the game board as the shepherd searches for his lost sheep. Parallel this game with the parable and how much God keeps looking for us when we have strayed away from Him.

What you need:

tagboard   clear contact paper (optional)

cardboard   colored markers or crayons

What you do:

• Copy and mount on tagboard the Lost Sheep Game Cards. You may want to color each shape a different color to help the children while playing. Be sure the same color is used for each shape. You may want to laminate with clear contact paper. Cut out the squares.

• Copy and mount the Lost Sheep gameboard onto a file folder. If you colored the game cards, you will need to color the gameboard to correspond with the cards. Laminating is recommended but not necessary.

• Copy and mount on cardboard the gameboard markers. To differentiate players, each stand should be a different color or copied onto colored paper.

How to play:

• Each player chooses a gameboard marker (sheep). Shuffle and stack the playing cards and set them on the gameboard. The first player (usually the youngest) draws a card and moves to the first square with that shape or picture. Double shapes on a card means that a player can move ahead two of that shape. More than one player can occupy a square at one time.

• The picture cards must be followed, as you may end up going back to help the shepherd search in the bushes!

Winning the game:

- The child who reaches the shepherd with a square playing card first is the winner. Players can only move if there is an available square to match their playing card at the end of the game.

How to store your game:

- Attach an envelope to the outside of a file folder (glue works well), The playing cards and gameboard markers should be stored in the envelope. Your whole game is now together for easy storage.

The Parable of the Lost Sheep Game

Lost Sheep Game Cards

"Oh no!" One sheep is missing!	Was the sheep under a bush?	Was the sheep on a hillside?	The Shepherd looked all night.
Was the sheep between two rocks?	◯	◯	◯
◯	▭	▭	▭
▭	△	△	△
△	□	□	▭ ▭
□	□ □	◯ ◯	△ △

The Parable of the Lost Sheep Game
Gameboard Markers

Copy and mount on tagboard. Cut out sheep on dotted lines. Cut stands on solid lines. cut slit in sheep (solid line) and slide onto stand to make your gameboard marker. Color each stand a different color.

God rejoices whenever one person asks for forgiveness and Jesus to live in their heart!

You found the lost sheep!

START

GAME CARDS

Who/What Bible Bingo

All ages

A test of Bible knowledge. This Who/What Bible Bingo game asks a question that the players must know the answer to in order to put their marker on their Who/What Bible Bingo game card. Great for early readers as well as people of all ages.

What you need:
- Prepare game set-up as instructed in Bible Picture Bingo (see page 26).
  Bingo Cards (pages 122-131)
  Caller's cards (pages 132-133)
  Bingo Master Card (pages 134-135)

What you do:
- The caller however must be able to read. When the caller draws the caller's cards and reads the statement or question out loud, those playing must find the corresponding answer on their bingo card.

- Decide before the game starts whether answers will be given during play or after the game is over. If it is decided that the answers will not be given during play, the players cannot put their marker on their card if they do not know the appropriate answer.

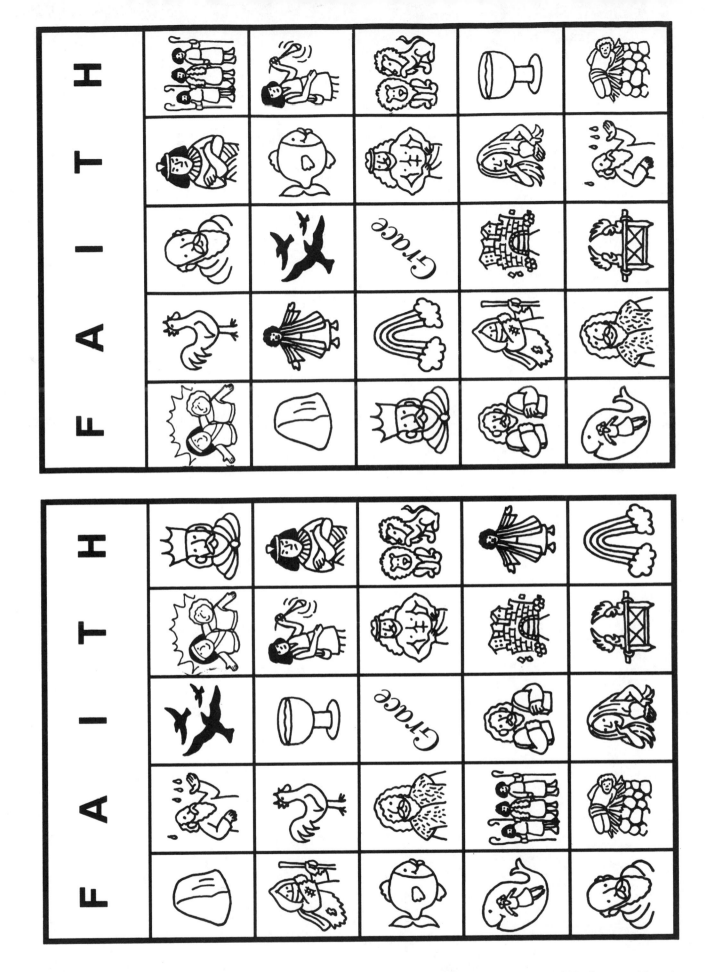

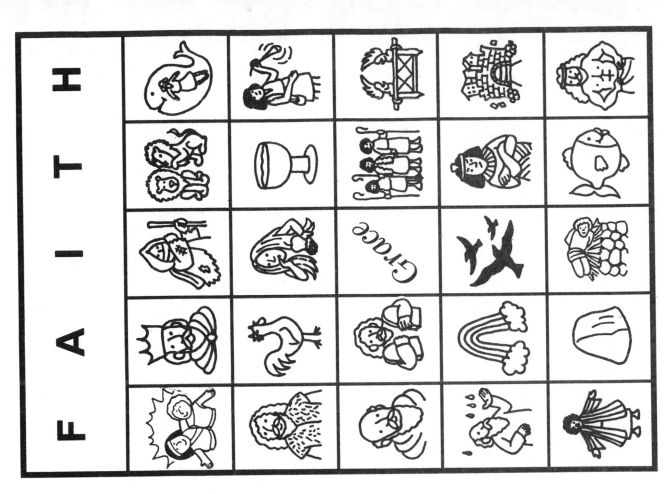

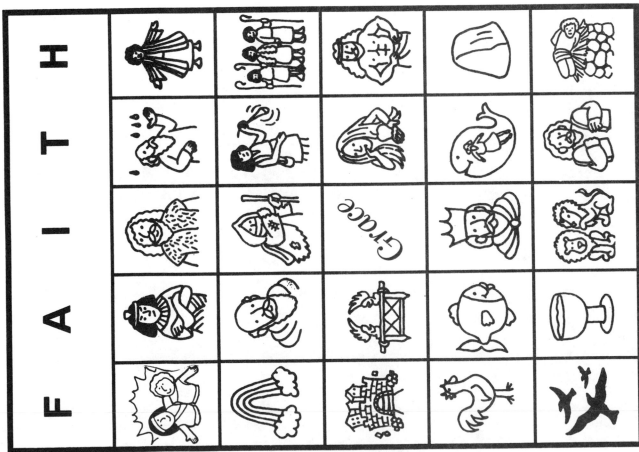

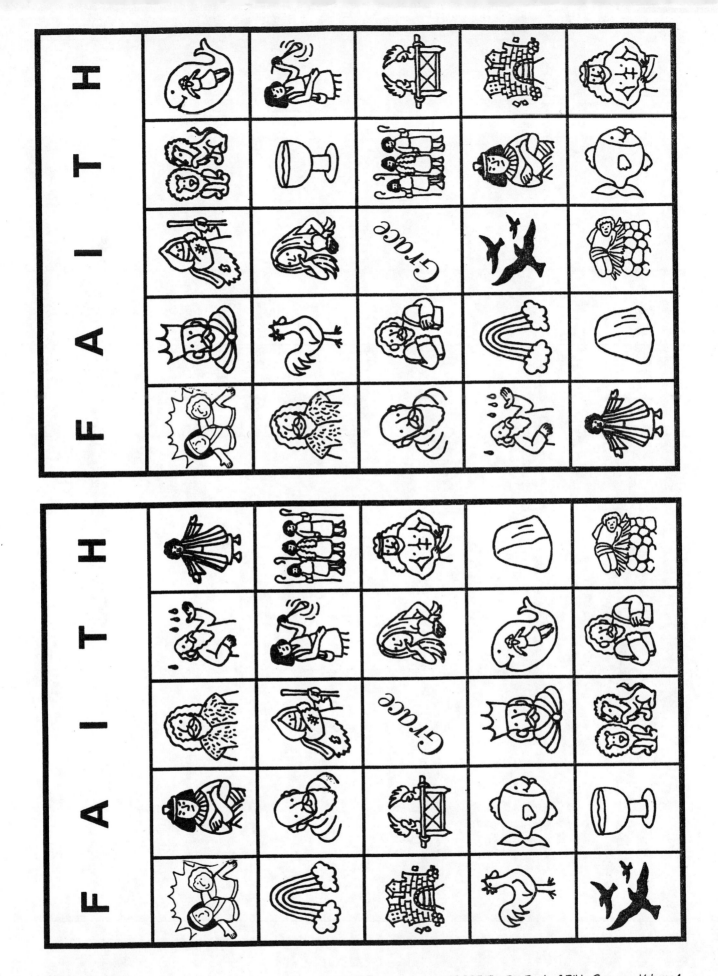

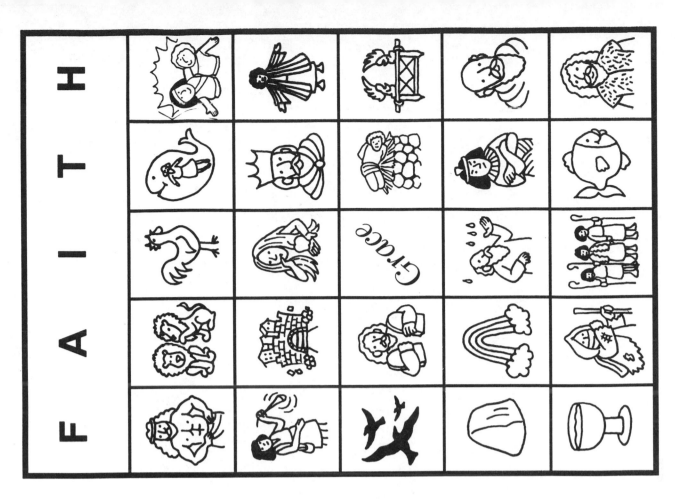

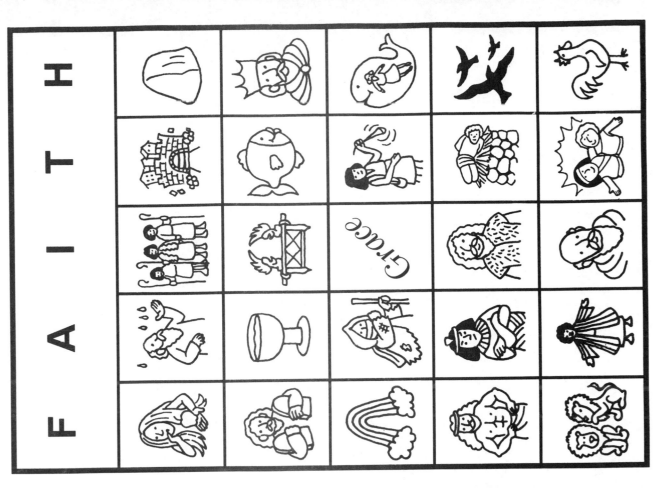

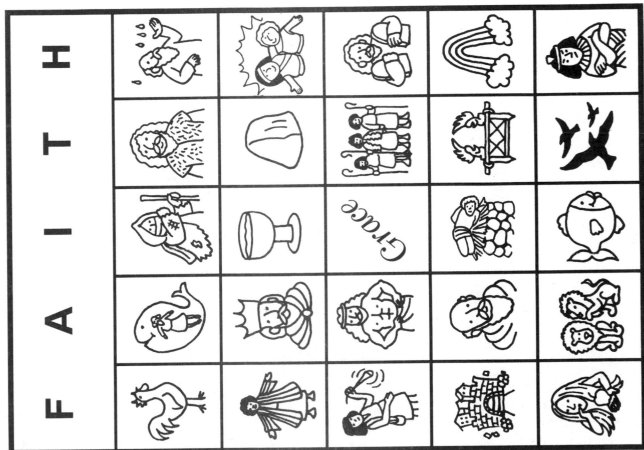

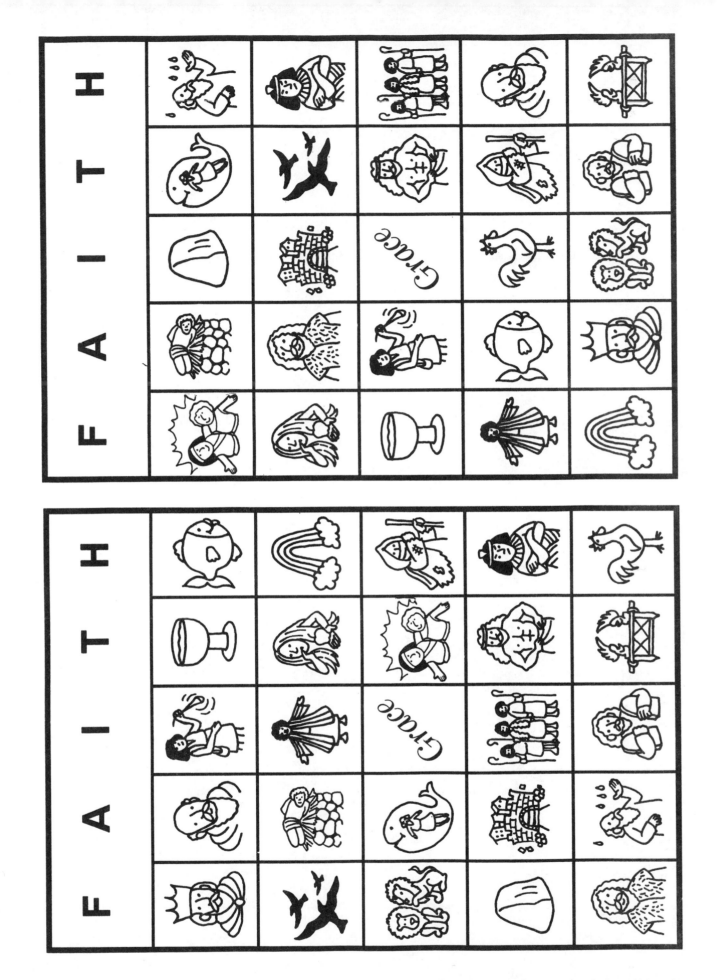

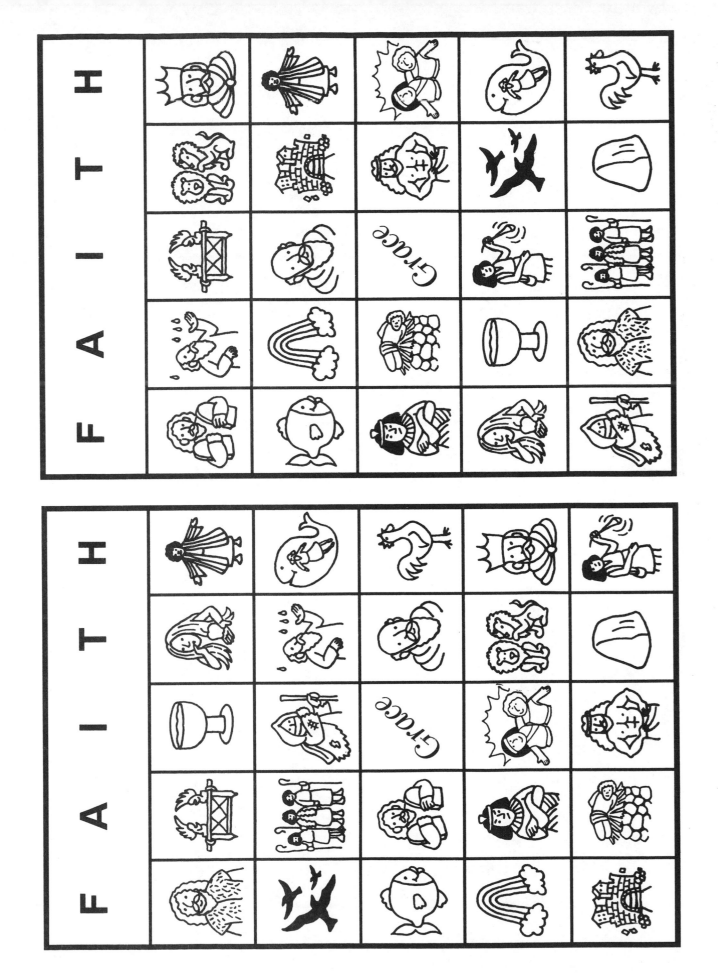

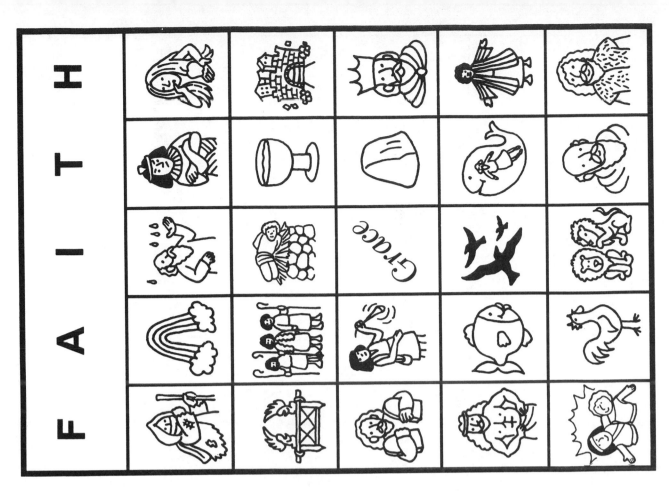

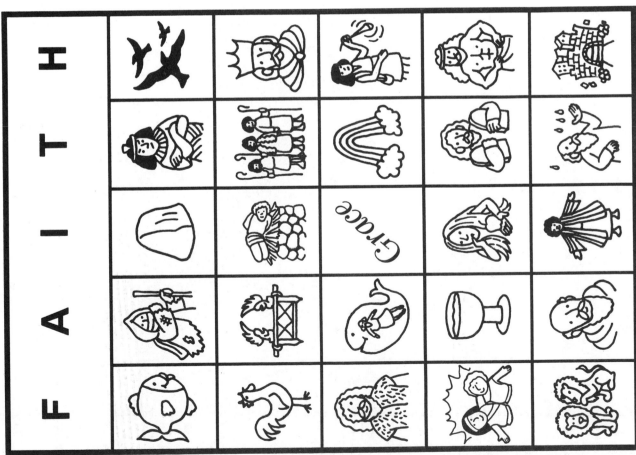

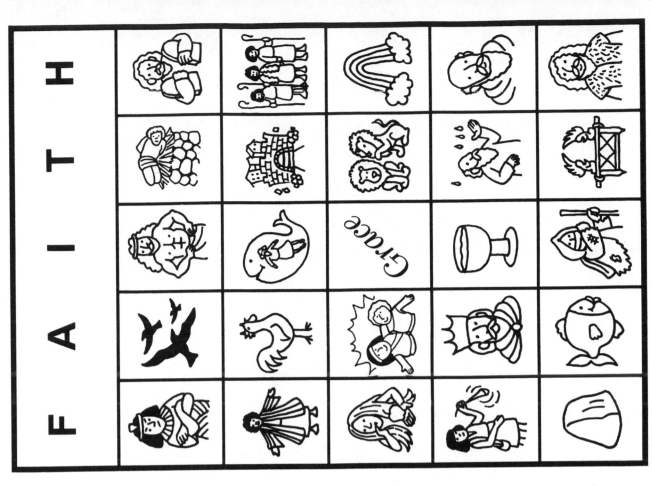

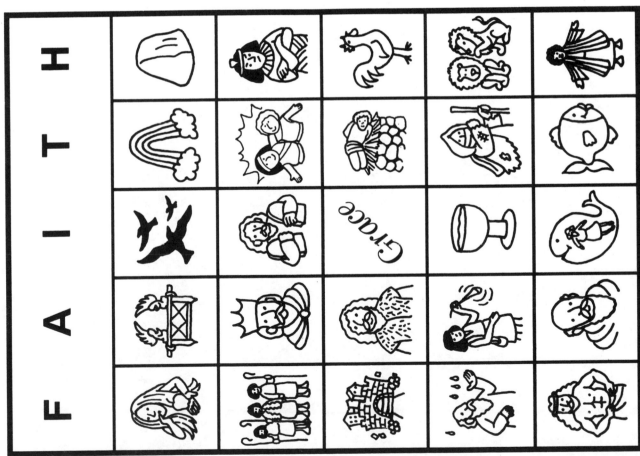

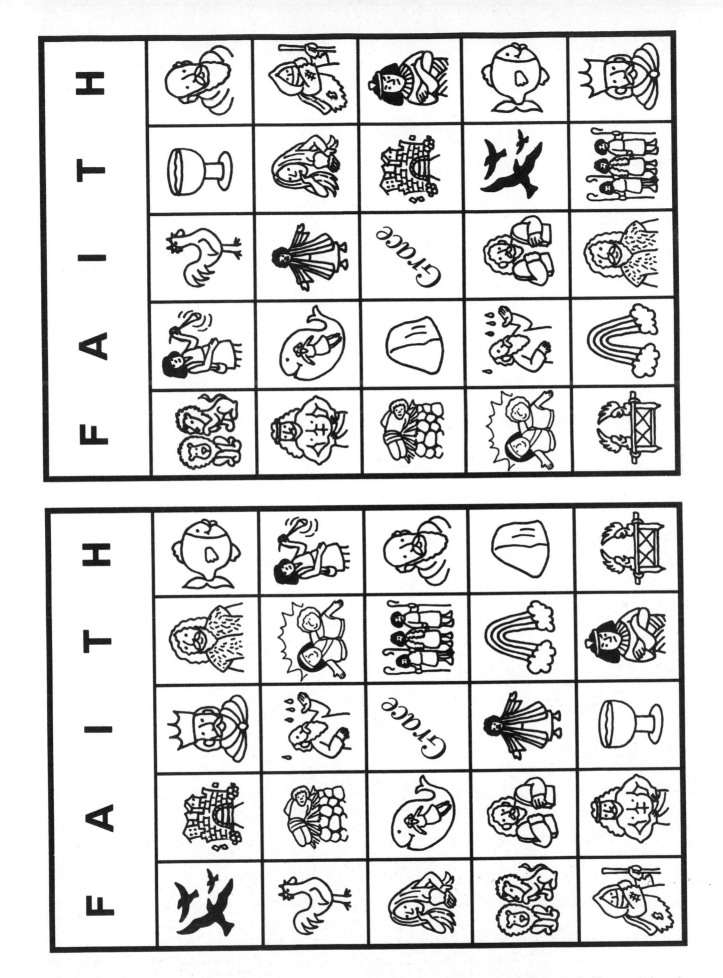

Who/What Bingo Calling Cards

Q: You should build your house upon a ___. A: Rock	Q: All I needed was a slingshot. A: David	Q: Jesus healed ten men with this disease. A: Leprosy	Q: Jesus used a few ___ and loaves of bread to feed 5,000 people. A: Fish	Q: Who baptized Jesus? A: John the Baptist
Q: Do unto others as you want them to do unto you. What is this called? A: The Golden Rule	Q: Who prayed for wisdom? A: Solomon	Q: What crowed three times while Peter denied knowing Jesus? A: Rooster	Q: Jesus turned water into ___. A: Wine	Q: An angel woke ___ to tell that a king had been born. A: Shepherds

Q: What is God's covenant of love? A: A rainbow	**Q: Who went up to heaven in a whirlwind?** A: Elijah	**Q: What city fell at a trumpet blast?** A: Jericho	**Q: Who did God ask to build the ark?** A: Noah
Q: Name the chest where the Ten Commandments were placed. A: Ark of the Covenant	**Q: Who was put in a basket in a river?** A: Moses	**Q: God sent these to feed Elijah.** A: Ravens	**Q: Who did the snake tell to eat the apple?** A: Eve
Grace	**Q: Abraham and Sarah are my parents.** A: Isaac	**Q: The big fish spit me out.** A: Jonah	**Q: God kept these mouths closed for Daniel.** A: Lions
			Q: I had a dream that my brothers would bow down to me. A: Joseph

Q: Who did not want to free Moses and his people?

A: Pharaoh

Q: My hair is my strength. Who am I?

A: Samson

Who/What Bible Bingo Master Card

FAITH

Ark of the Covenant	Shepherds
The Golden Rule	Joseph
Wine	Jericho
David	Samson
Solomon	Jonah

continued on next page

overlap page xx onto this section and glue

Elijah		Grace
Lions	Ravens	Fish
A rainbow	Moses	Noah
Leprosy	Rock	Pharaoh
Eve	John the Baptist	Isaac

Preparation of game:
- Copy the nine pages of the ark and mount on tagboard. You may want to paint or color the ark. Laminate with clear contact paper.
- Cut out and color the pictures of the animals. You may want to laminate them with clear contact paper.

Object of the game:
- To pin the animal the closest to the door of the ark while wearing a blindfold.

Materials needed:
tagboard   tape
scissors   clear contact paper
bandanna   ark pattern (pages 144-153)
people and animal patterns (pages 137-143)

To play:
- Hang the picture of the ark at child's level on a wall.
- Blindfold the first player and have that child try to pin (or tape) an animal in the doorway of the ark. (You can roll tape on the back to make it stick.)
- Everyone gets a chance to pin an animal on the doorway of the ark.

Pin the Animals on the Ark Animals

Pin the Animals on the Ark Animals

Pin the Animals on the Ark Animals

Pin the Animals on the Ark Animals

Pin the Animals on the Ark Animals

Pin the Animals on the Ark Animals

Pin the Animals on the Ark Animals

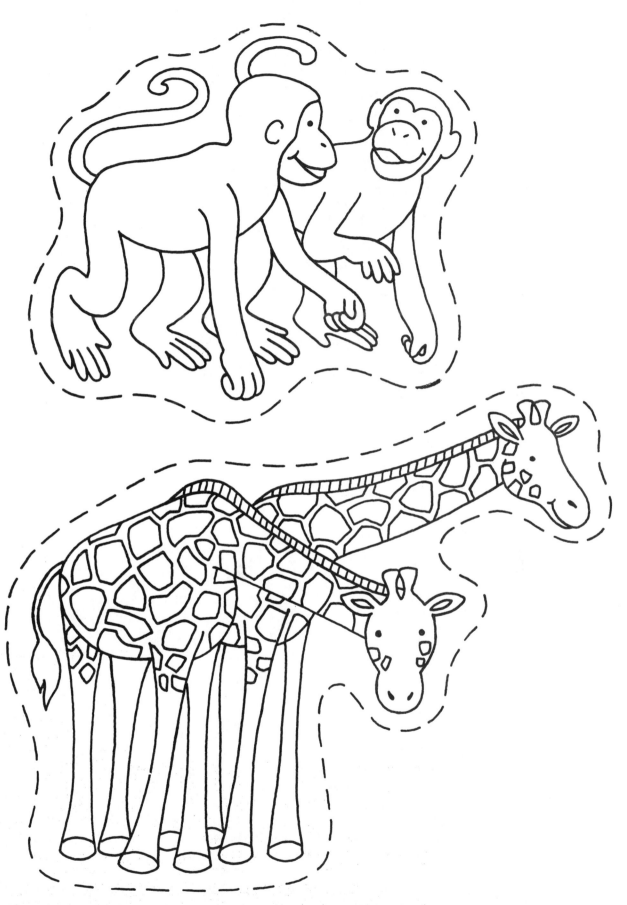

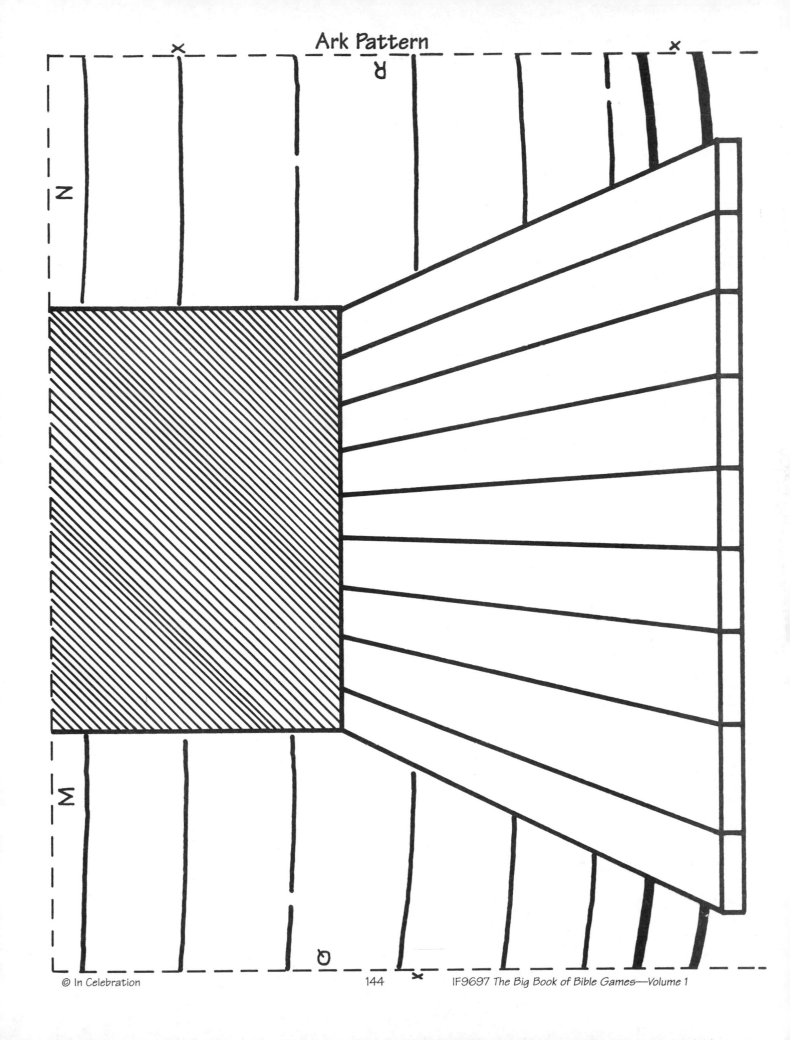

Ark Pattern

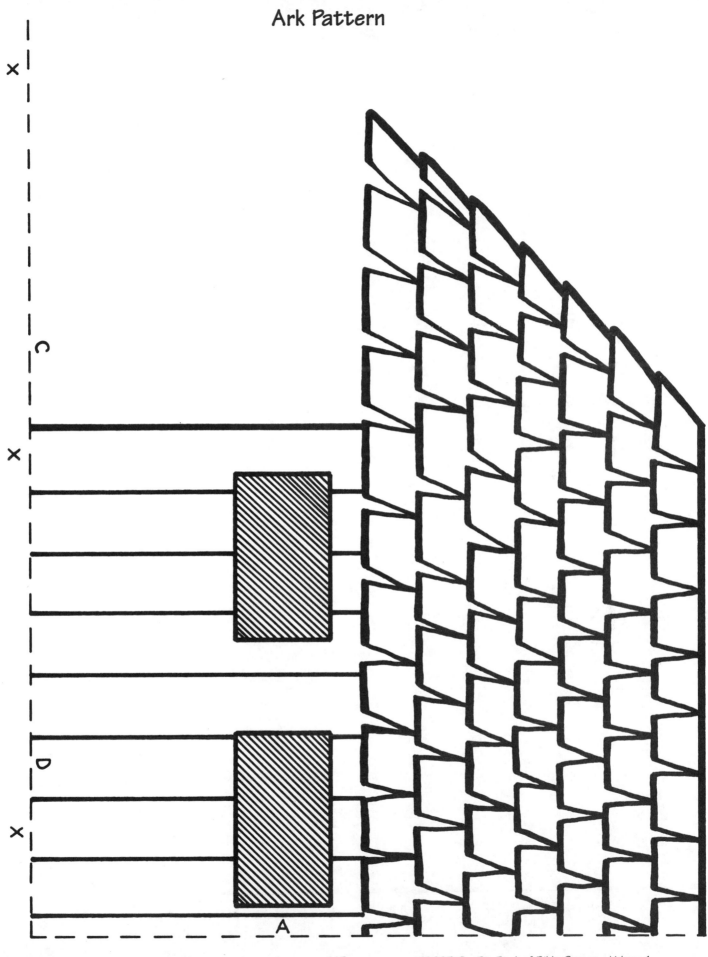

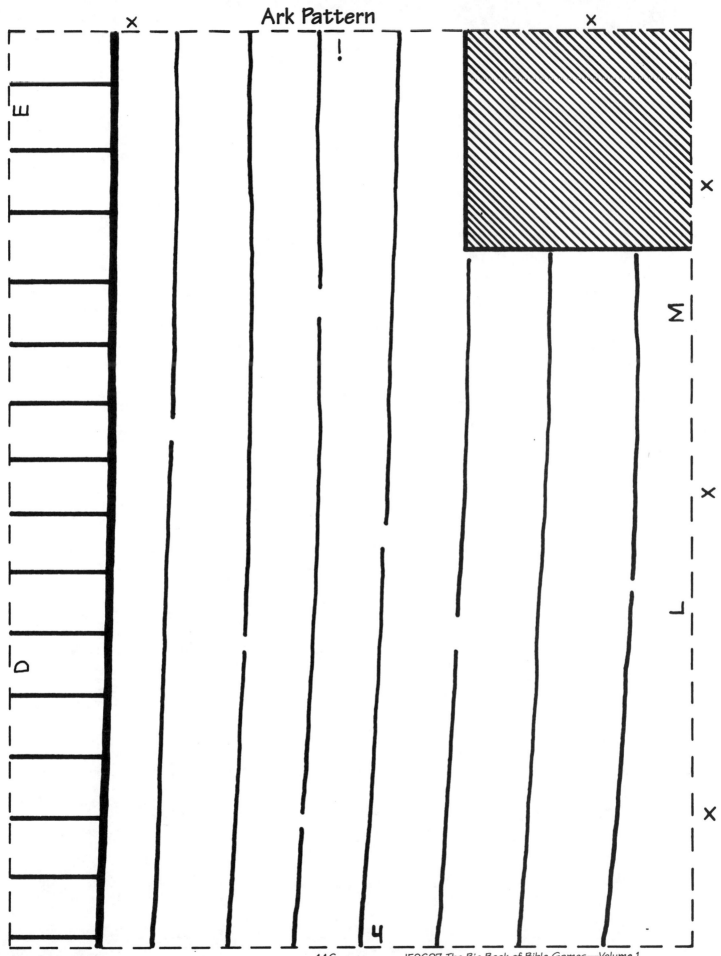

Ark Pattern

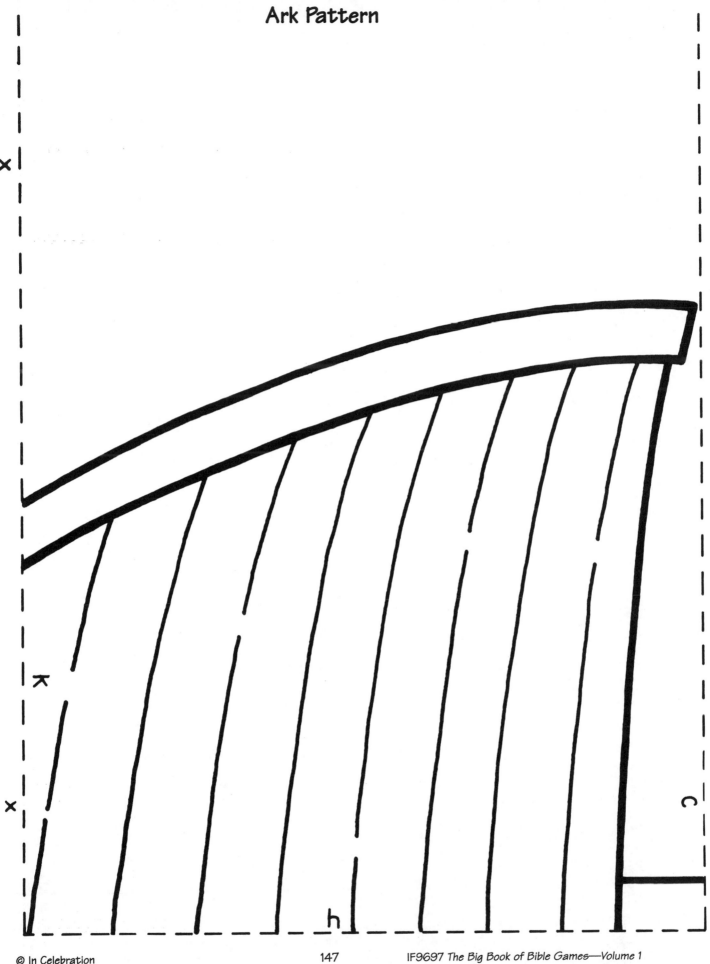

Ark Pattern

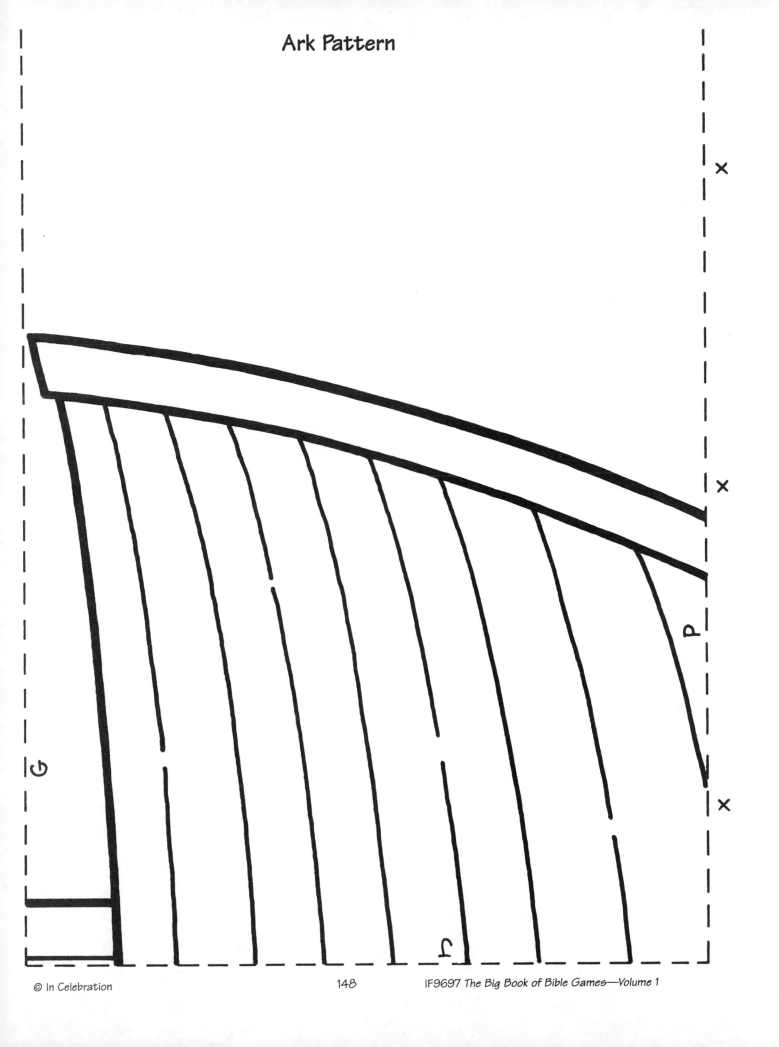

Ark Pattern

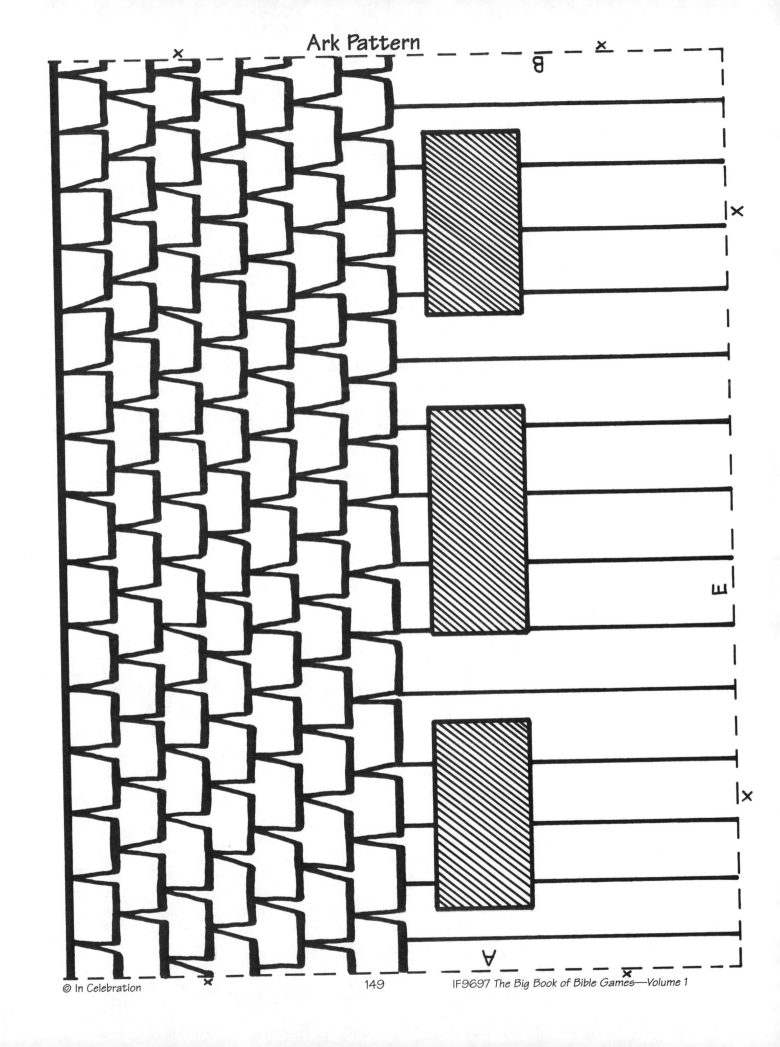

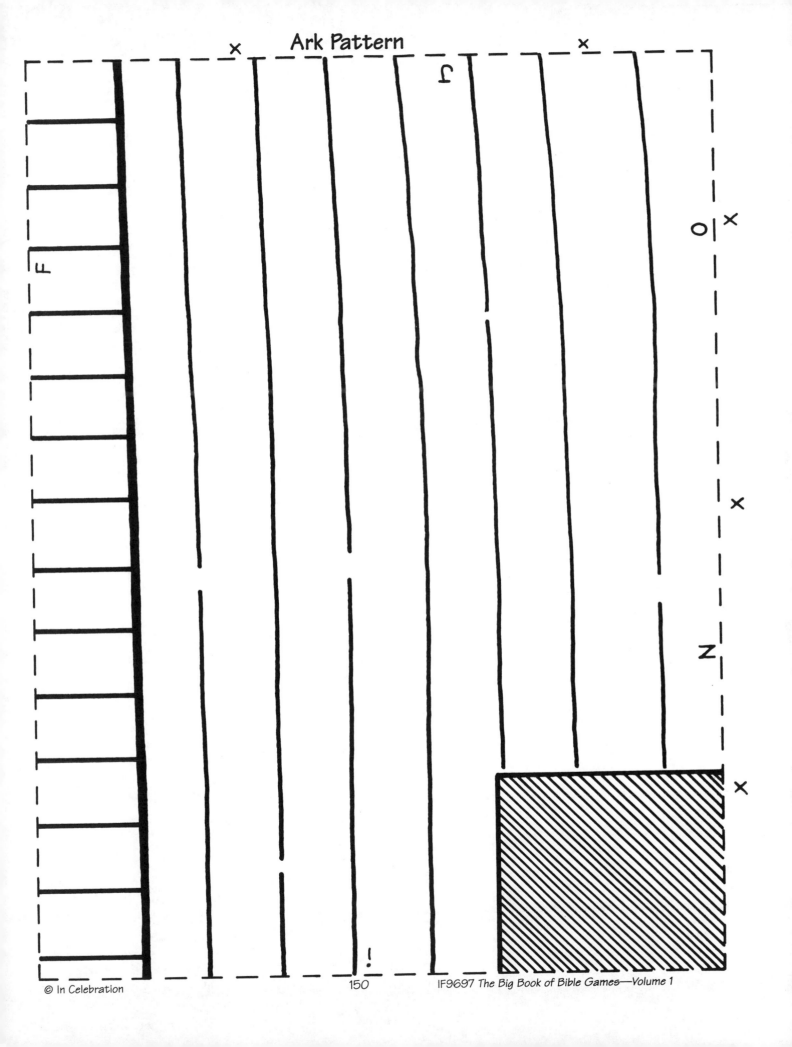

Ark Pattern

Ark Pattern

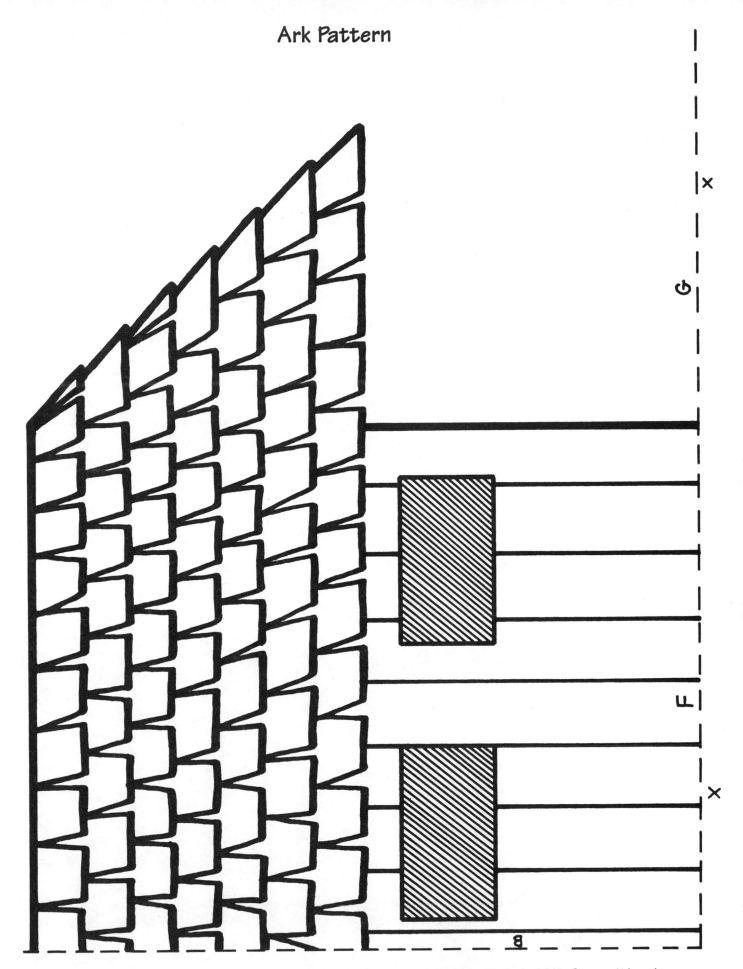

Ark Pattern

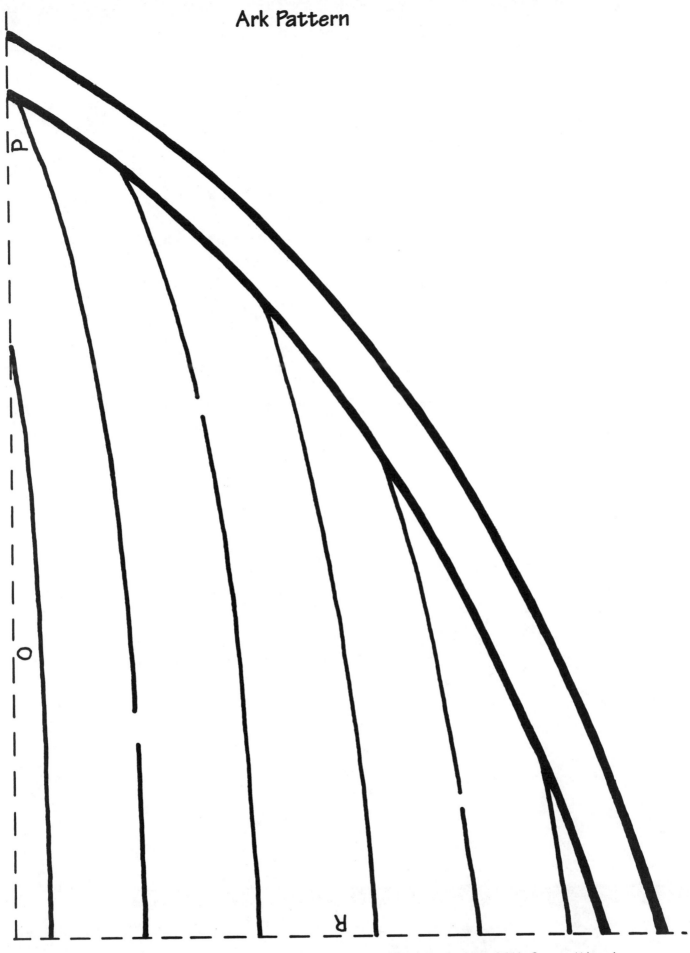

152

Ark Pattern

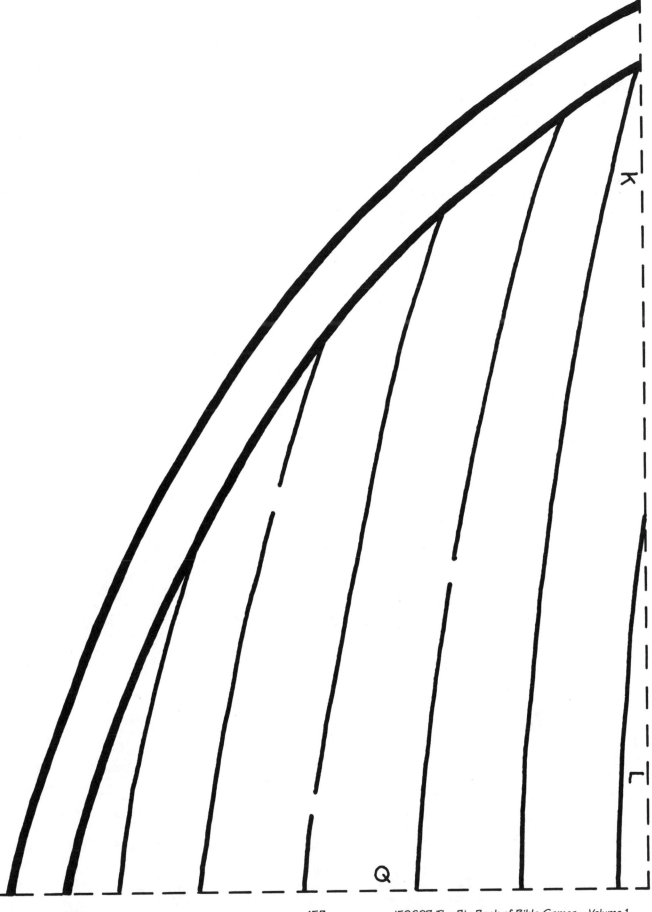

K

L

Q

Picture Pairs Card Game
All ages (4–8 players)

Preparation of game:
- Copy two sets of the game cards (patterns are found on pages 155-159). Be sure that you have created two of every card - except the "Pilate" card.
- Color the playing cards if desired, or copy on colored construction paper.
- Cut out and mount onto heavier paper or tagboard. Laminate with clear contact paper.
- Before playing the game, discuss with the children the pictures that go together. Explain that the "Pilate" card does not have a match. This card stands alone.

Object of the game:
- The player who is not holding any cards and has the most matches wins the game.

Materials needed:
    construction paper or tagboard
    clear contact paper
    scissors
    crayons or markers

To play:
- Shuffle and deal all of the cards among the players.

- Each player holds the cards that are dealt without showing them to other players and makes matches. Place the matching pairs on the table.

- The player with the fewest matching pairs is Player 1 or choose someone to start the "play." Player 1 draws one card from another player's hand, looks at the card and makes a pair, if possible. If a match cannot be made the player keeps the card.

- Play continues to the left. The second player draws one card from another player's hand and tries to make a match or keeps the card.

- Play continues until a player is not holding any cards and has the most matches. That player is the winner. The player holding the "Pilate" card loses the game but gets to start the next game.

Daniel

Lions Den

David

Goliath

Samson

Delilah

Women

Lost Coin

Joshua

Adam

Eve

Noah
and family

Rainbow

Garden
of Eden

Snake

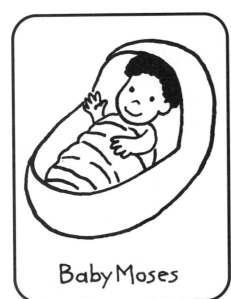

Baby Moses

Basket

Animals
2x2

Ark

Aaron
and Moses

Staff into
Snake

Adult Moses

Red Sea

Joseph

Colorful Coat

Jonah

Whale

Jericho

Baby Jesus

Manger

Shepherds

Angels Singing

Wisemen

Star

John

Baptized Jesus

Jesus' Death

Empty Tomb

Shepherd

Lost Sheep

Sower

Seed

Little Boy

2 fish and
5 loaves

Pilate

Solomon Says

Children can do action only when Solomon Says—otherwise the child is out.

Have children spread out—at least arms length from one another. The person who is Solomon faces the children so everyone can see and hear. Solomon is trying to catch people performing an action without the caller saying, "Solomon says . . ."

As you start the game, Solomon might say, "Solomon says jump up and down." All children jump up and down. Then Solomon might say, "Do a jumping jack." Solomon did **not** say, "Solomon says," and so all of those who did a jumping jack are out. Play continues until one child is left. The child who sins the first game becomes Solomon for the next game.

Bible Hot Potato

What you need:
> potato or ball and a whistle

Object of the game:
Be the last one remaining in the circle and win the game.

To play game:
Appoint a time keeper. Have children stand or sit in a circle. One is given a potato or a ball. A whistle is blown to designate the beginning of play—children must say a person from the Bible and throw the "hot potato" gently to another player. Players cannot repeat a Bible character's name, but must say another name and get rid of the "hot potato." The timer can go off at anytime. The player with the whistle turns his back to the game during play and can blow the whistle whenever she/he chooses. When the whistle blows again the person holding the potato or ball is out and must leave the circle. Play ends when only one person remains in the circle.

Statue Tag

> Knowing characters from the Bible is the only way to survive this game.

Object of the game:
> To try and not get tagged.

To play game:
- Divide children into two teams. One team is "it." Set a time limit and then switch so the other team can be "it."
- When you are tagged you must freeze like a statue until someone from your team touches you. You then must say the name of someone in the Bible to get "unfrozen" and are then free to run again.

Pharaoh, Pharaoh, Moses

Similar to Duck, Duck, Grey Duck, children sit in a a big circle with enough space to run around the outside of the circle. One person is chosen to start the game. That child walks behind everyone tapping each person's head saying "Pharaoh." When the child has chosen someone to chase her/him, the child is tapped and the word "Moses" is said. The child chosen runs around the circle after the child who tapped him. If the child in front gets to the open spot in the circle before being caught, he/she sits down. If the chaser catches the runner, the runner goes in the middle of the circle until a new game is started.